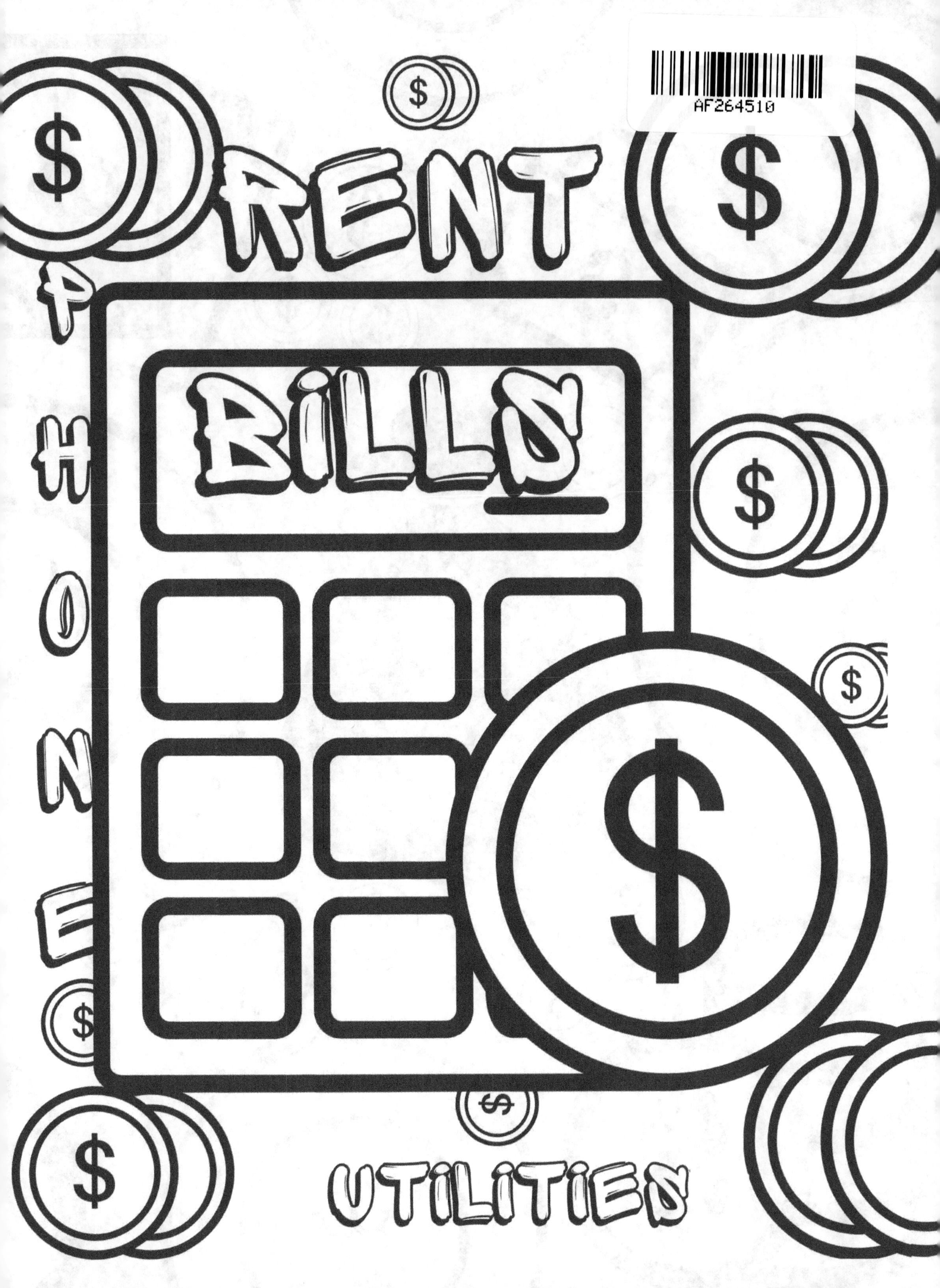

RENT
BILLS
PHONE
UTILITIES
$

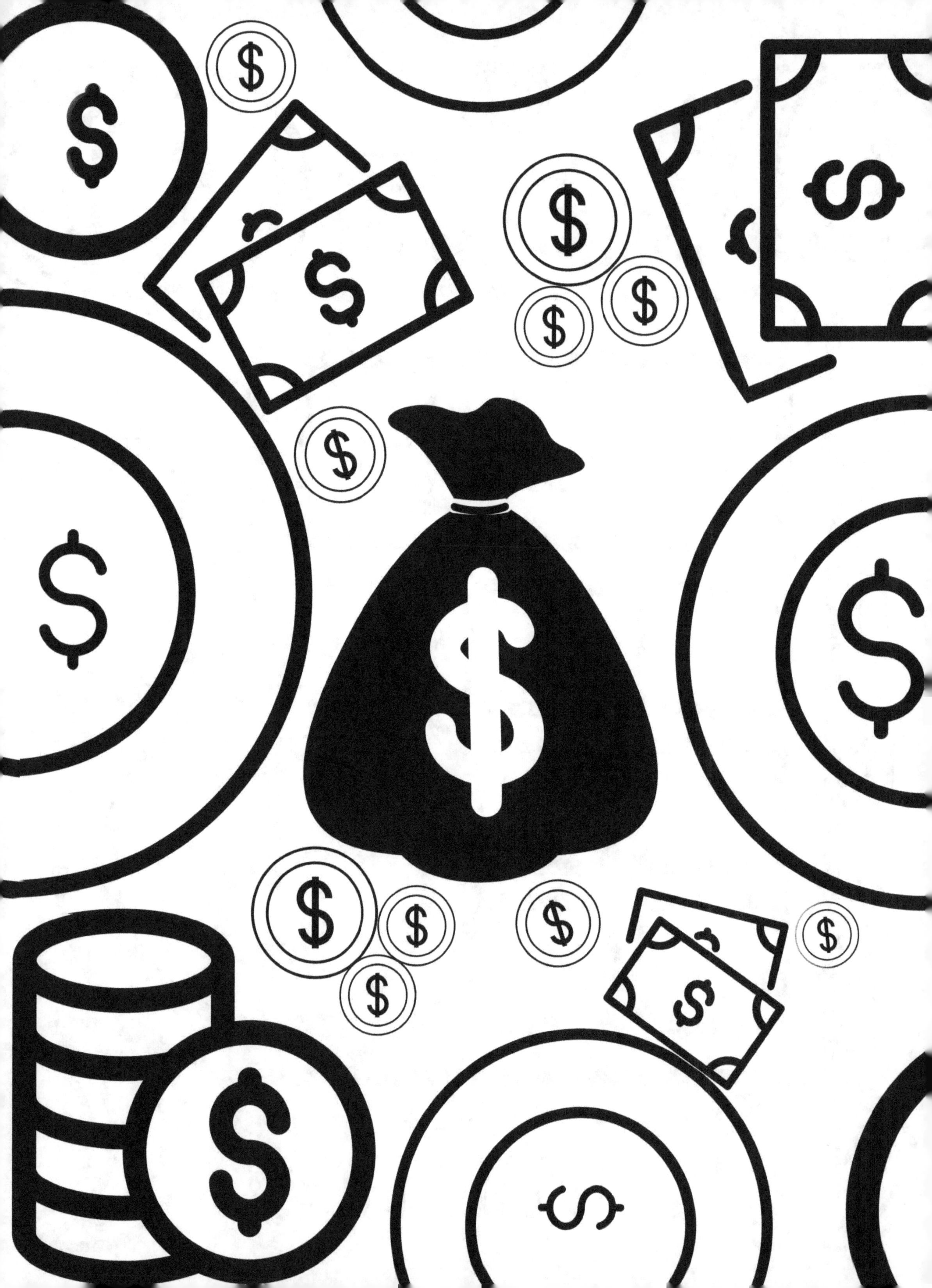

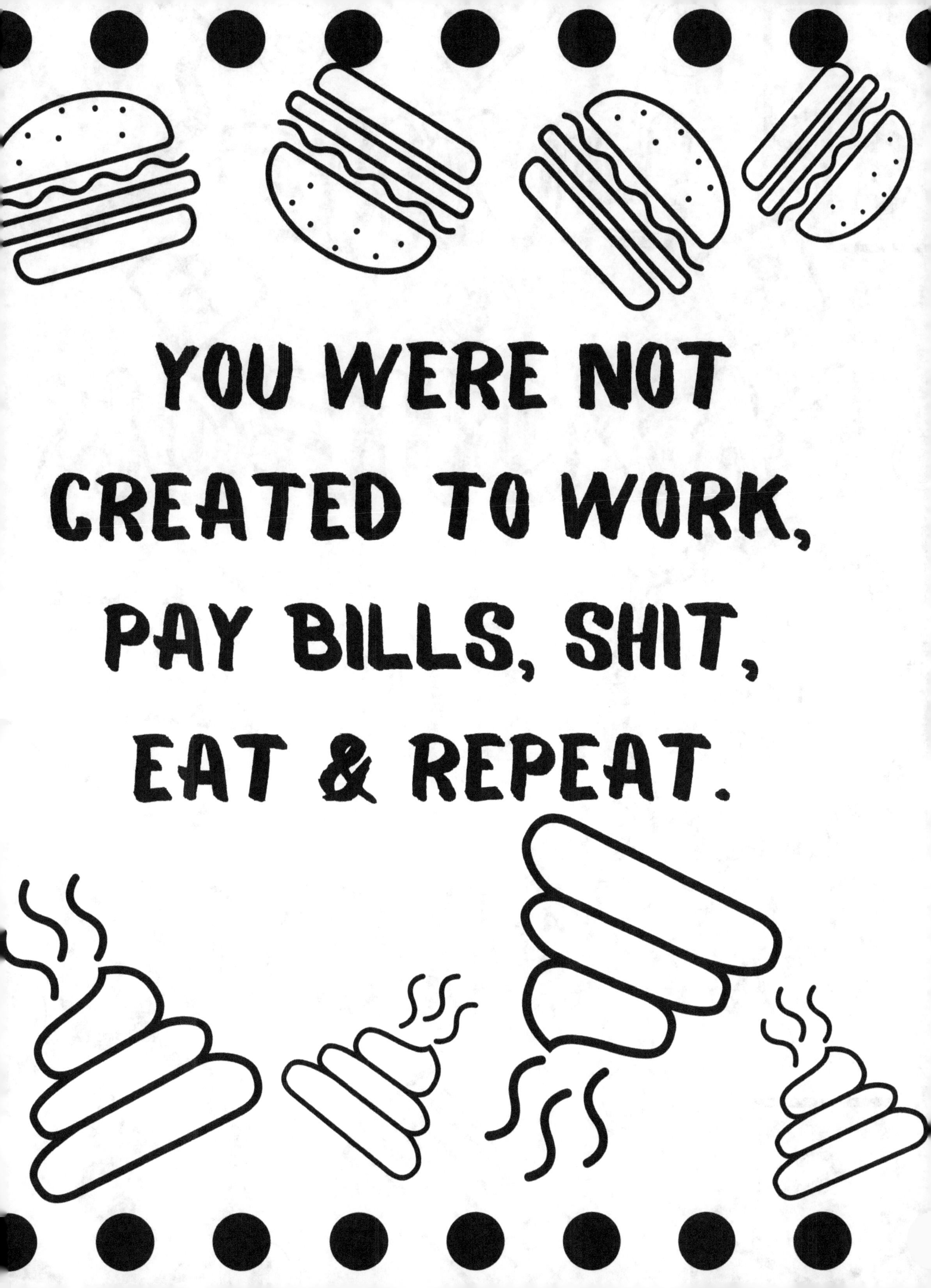

YOU WERE NOT
CREATED TO WORK,
PAY BILLS, SHIT,
EAT & REPEAT.

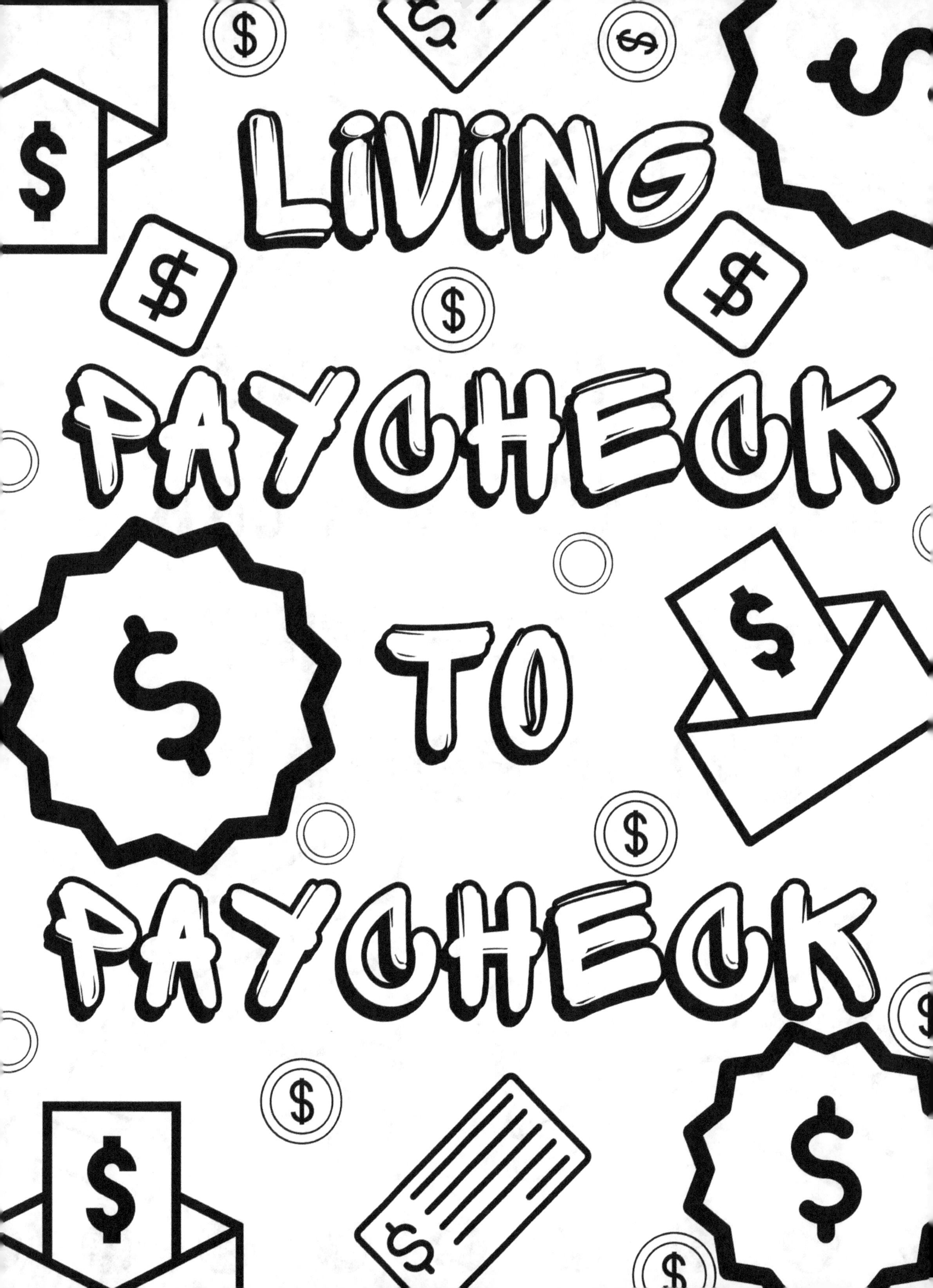

LIVING
PAYCHECK
TO
PAYCHECK

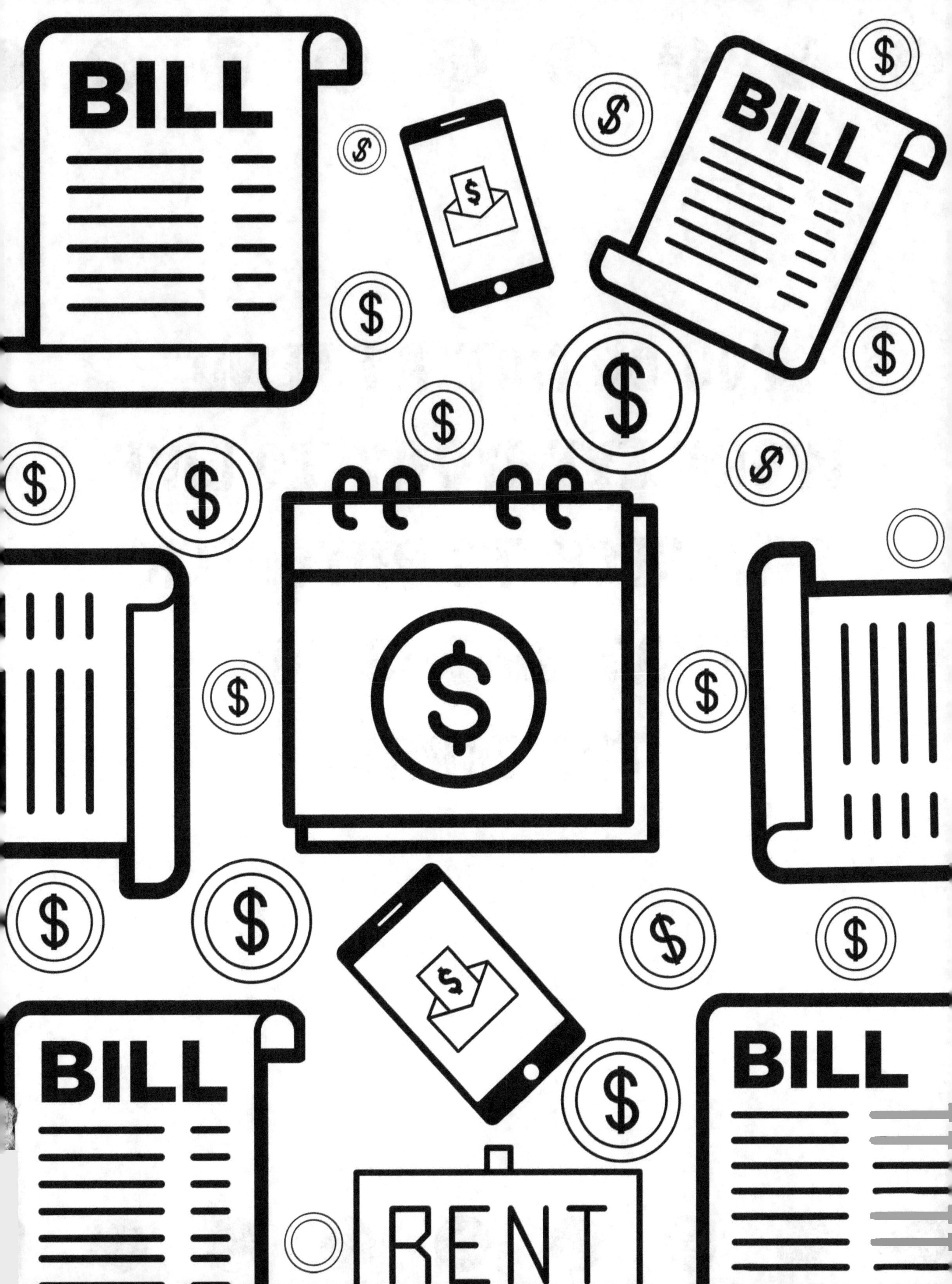

BILL
BILL
BILL
BILL
RENT

YOU DO NOT ATTEND
WORK EVERYDAY TO LIVE
PAYCHECK TO PAYCHECK.
THAT SHIT IS FOR
THE BIRDS!

WORK
SLAVING 40HRS
WORK
40HRS
WORK
FULL TIME
FULL TIME
WORK
FULL TIME
FULL TIME
MINIMUM PAY
WORK
WORK
WORK

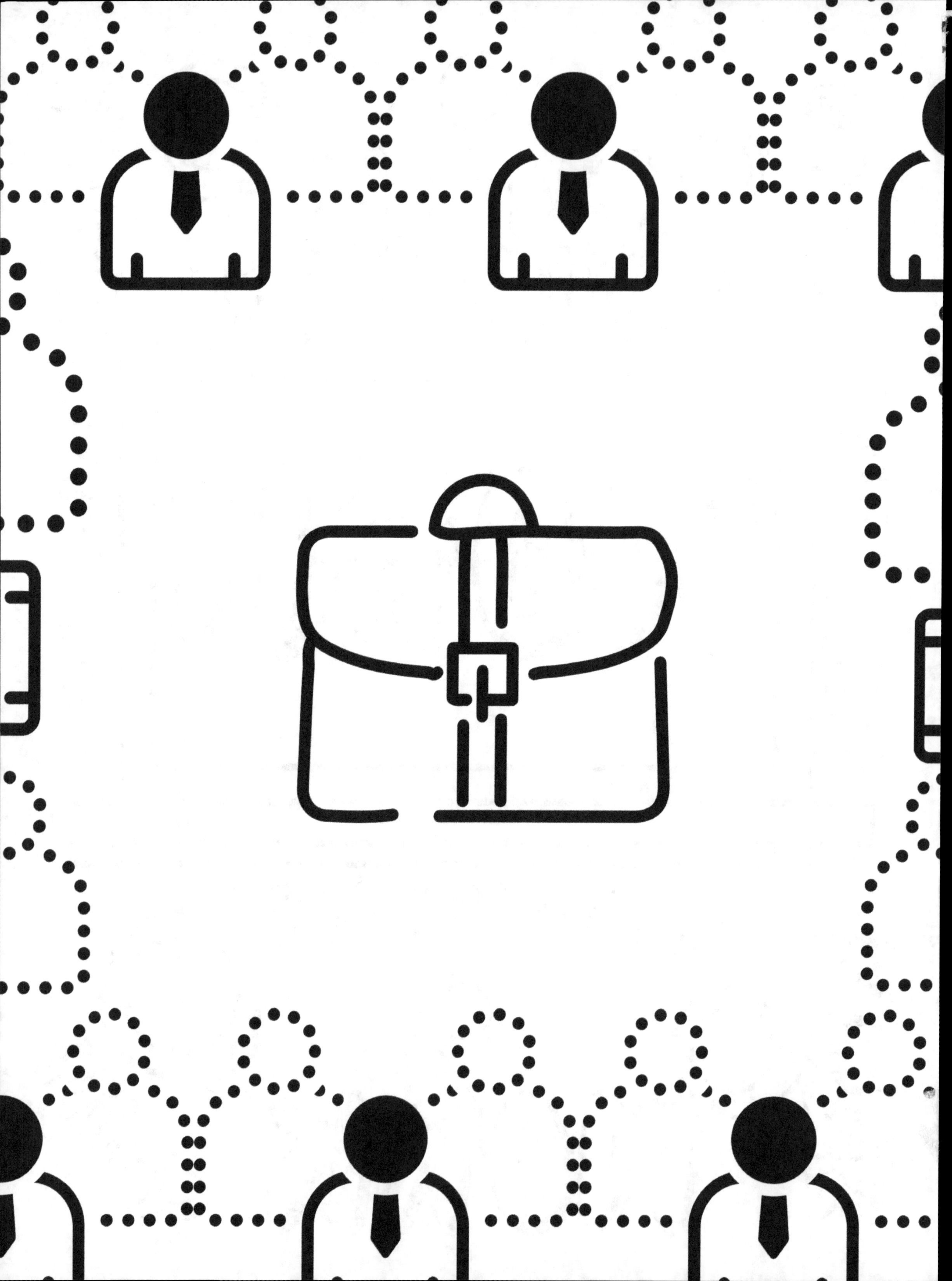

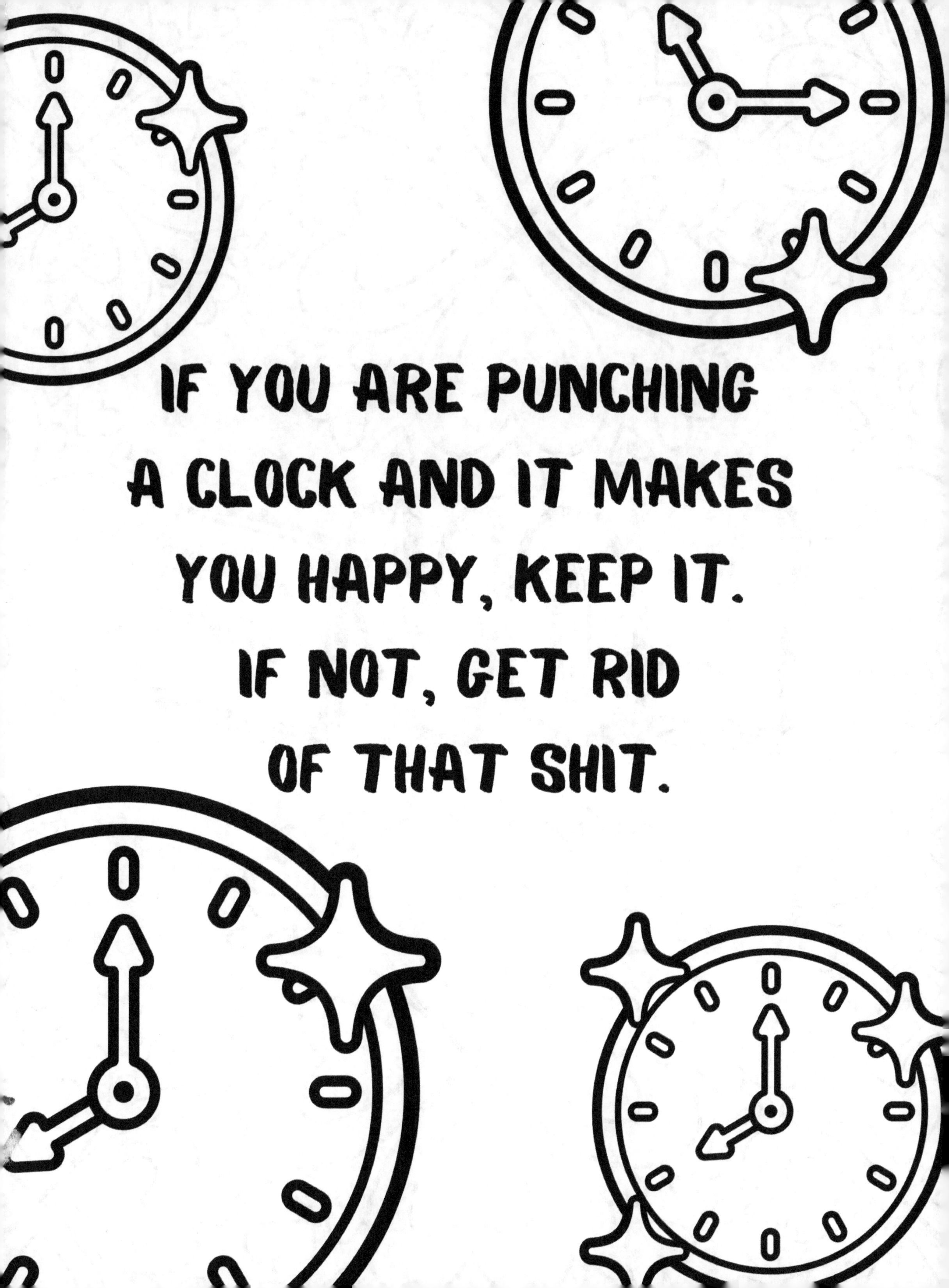
IF YOU ARE PUNCHING
A CLOCK AND IT MAKES
YOU HAPPY, KEEP IT.
IF NOT, GET RID
OF THAT SHIT.

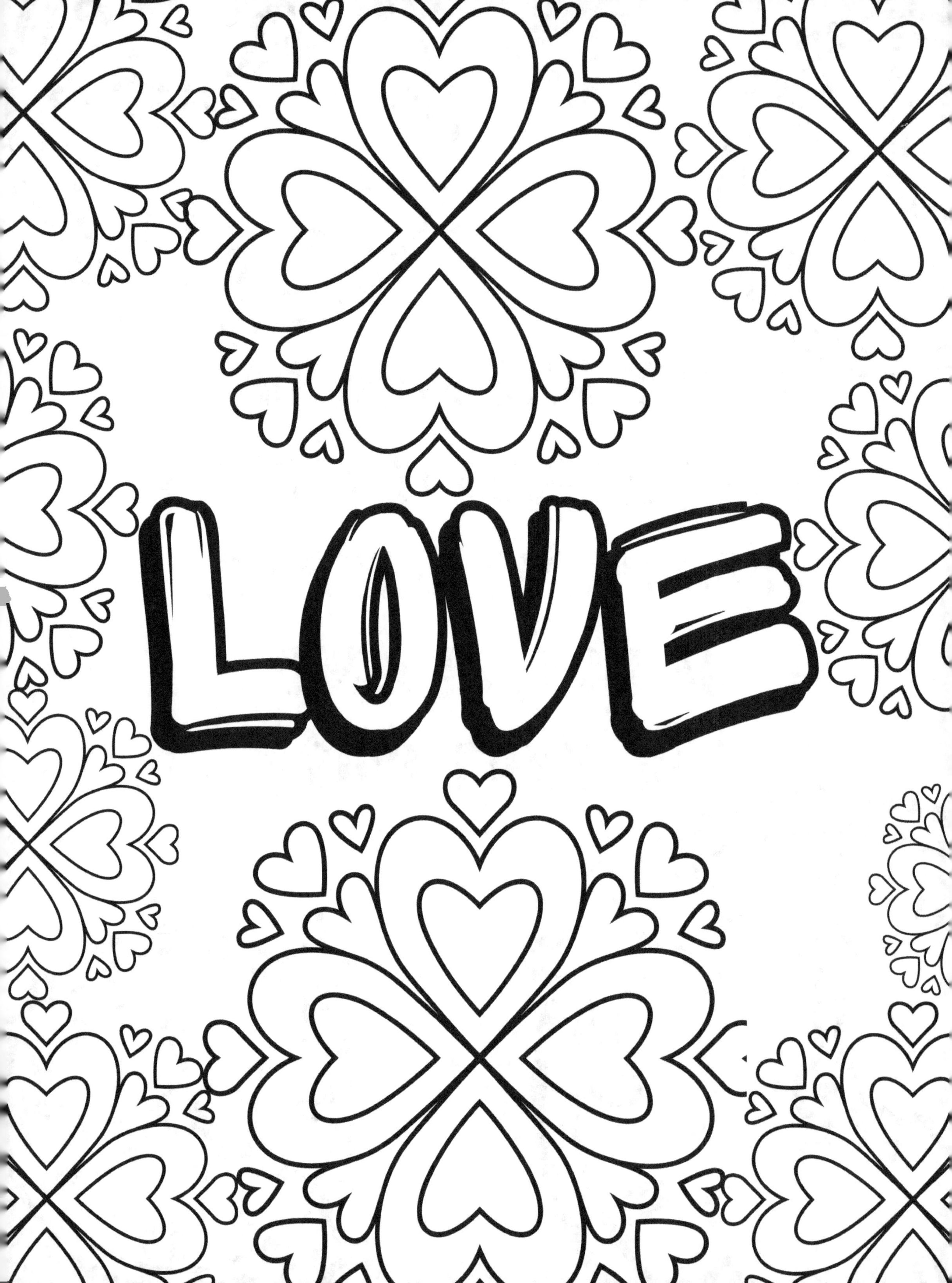
LOVE

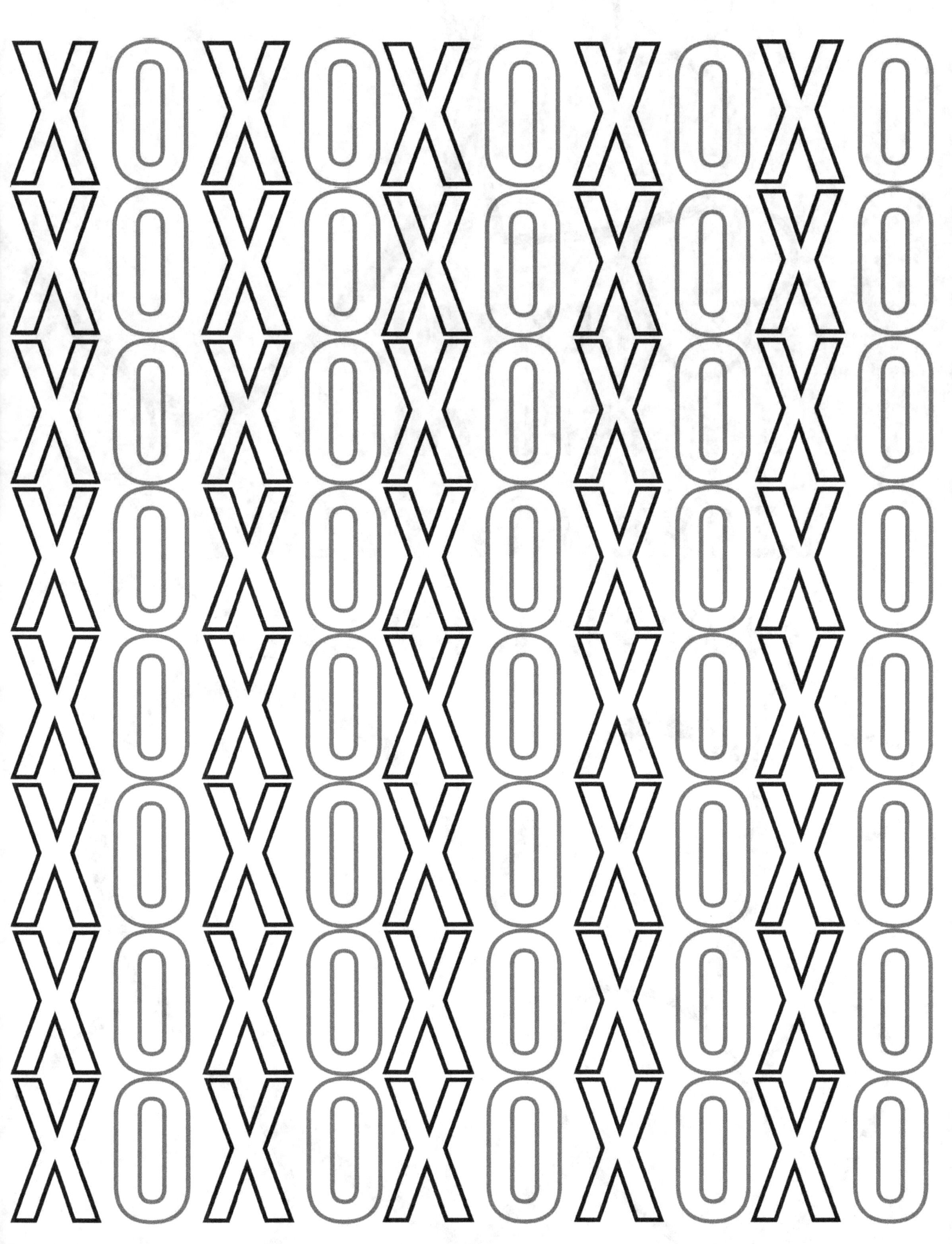

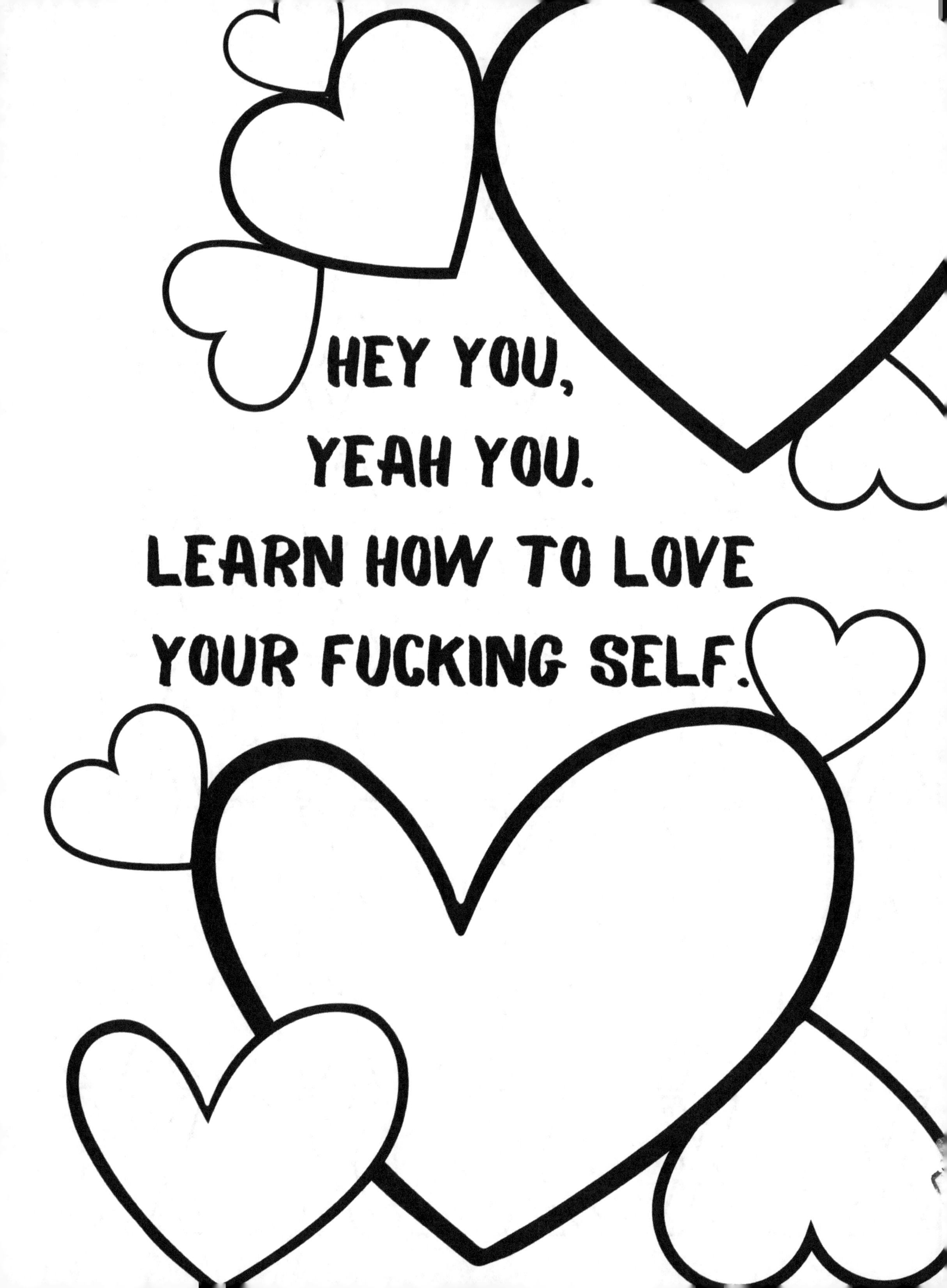

HEY YOU,
YEAH YOU.
LEARN HOW TO LOVE
YOUR FUCKING SELF.

EXISTING
AND
NOT LIVING

WHEN WRITING THE STORY
OF YOUR LIFE, DO NOT LET
SOMEONE ELSE HOLD THE PEN.

CRYING
IN
SILENCE

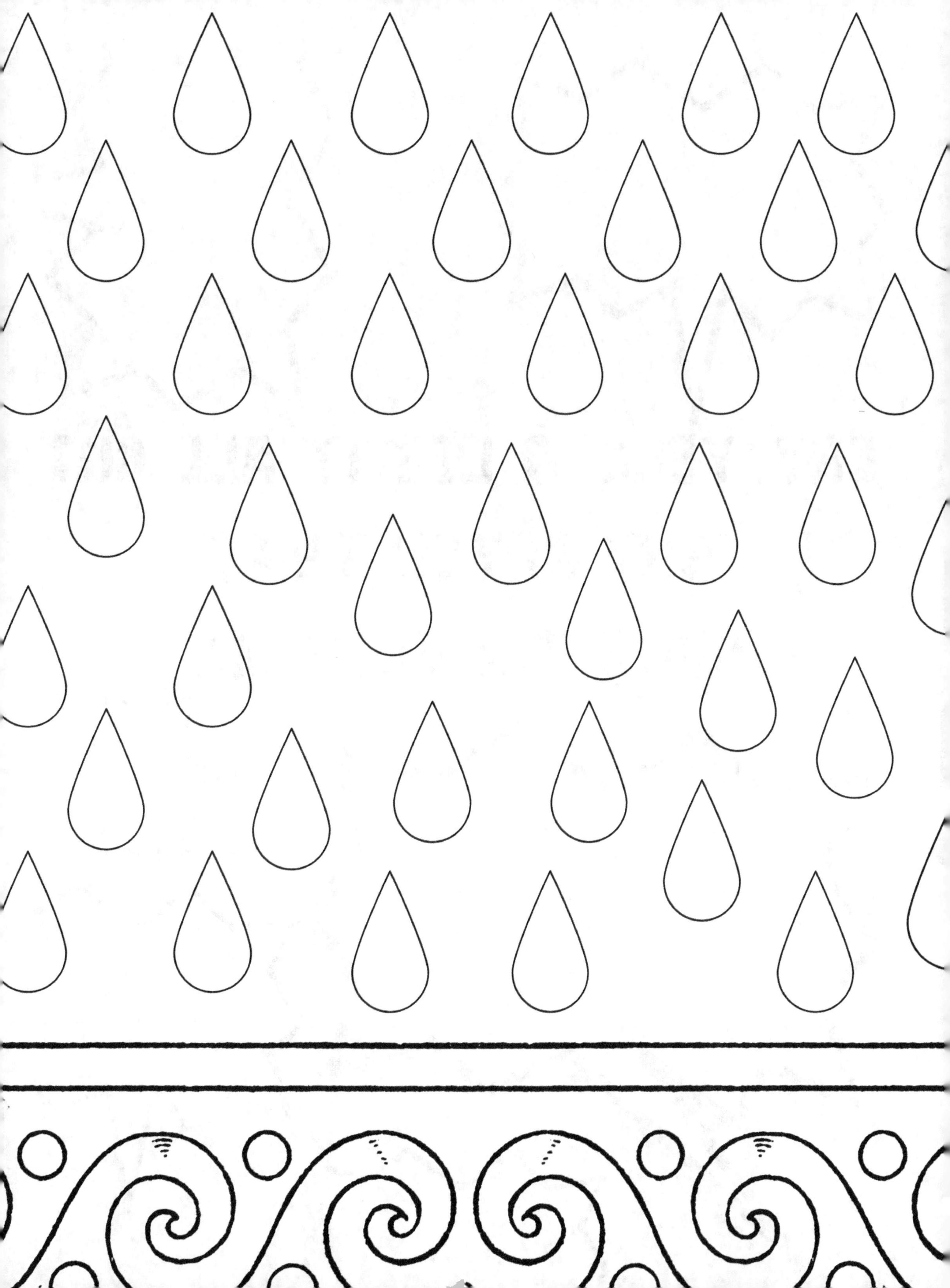

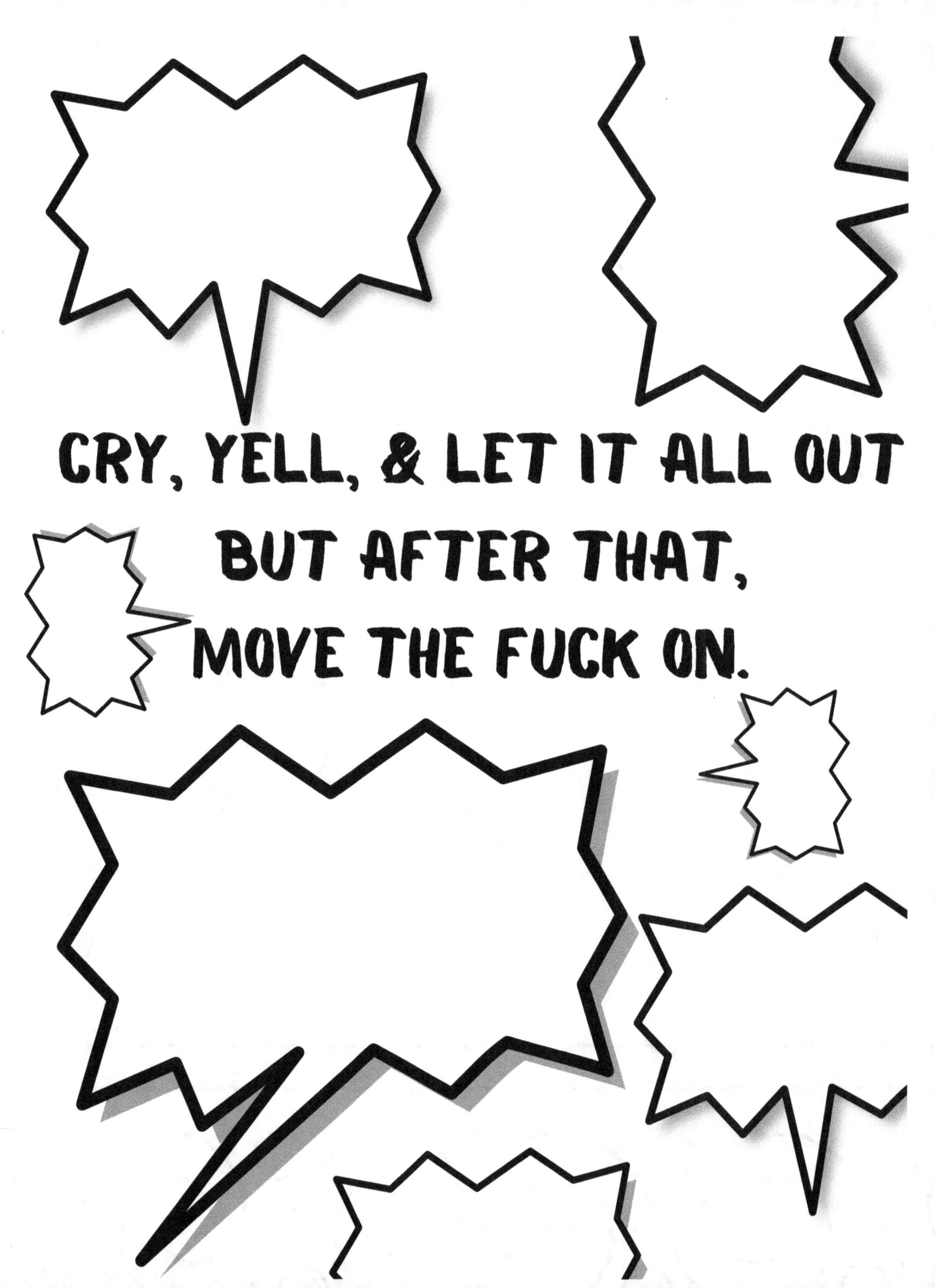

CRY, YELL, & LET IT ALL OUT
BUT AFTER THAT,
MOVE THE FUCK ON.

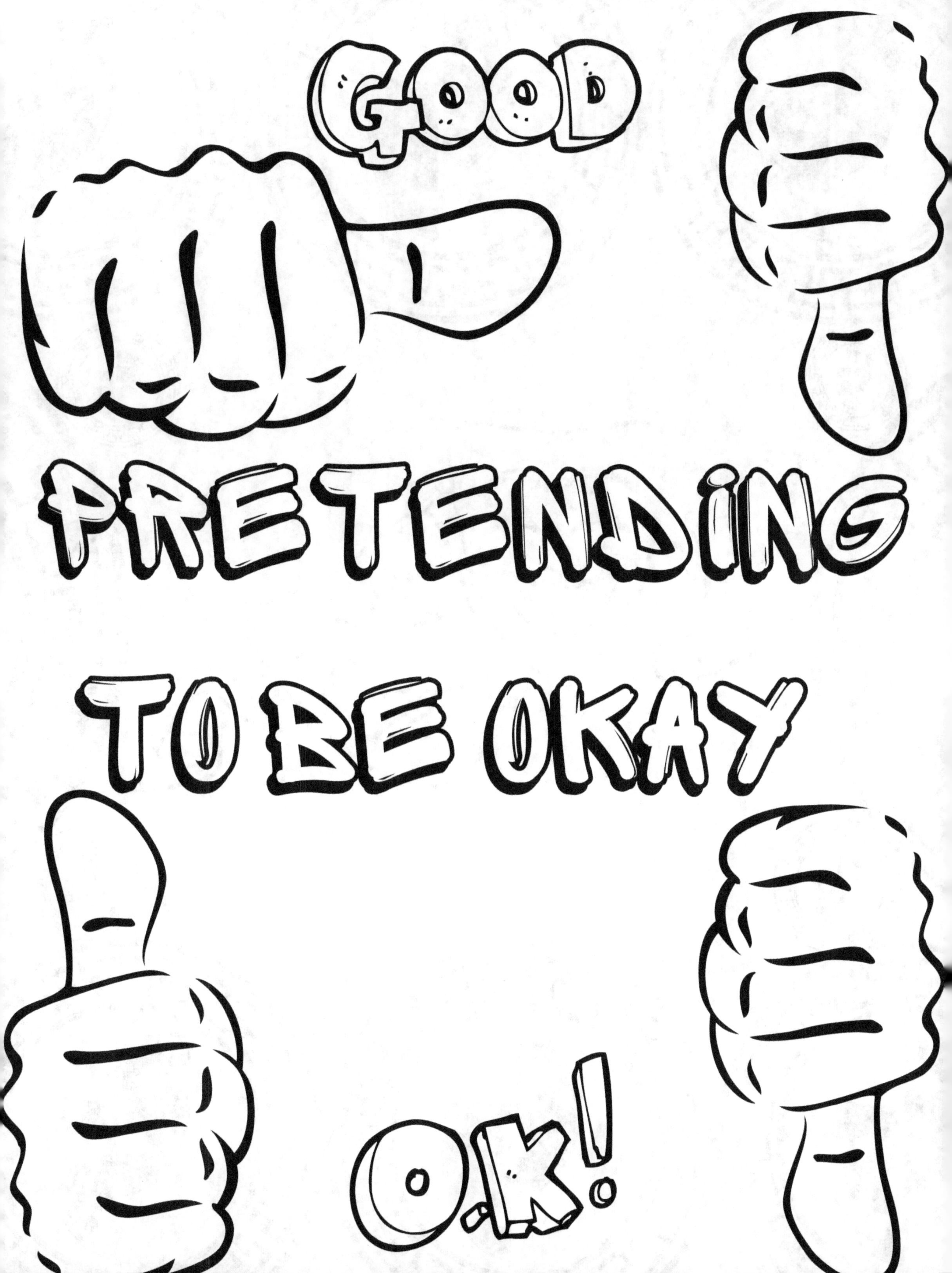

GOOD
PRETENDING
TO BE OKAY
O.K!

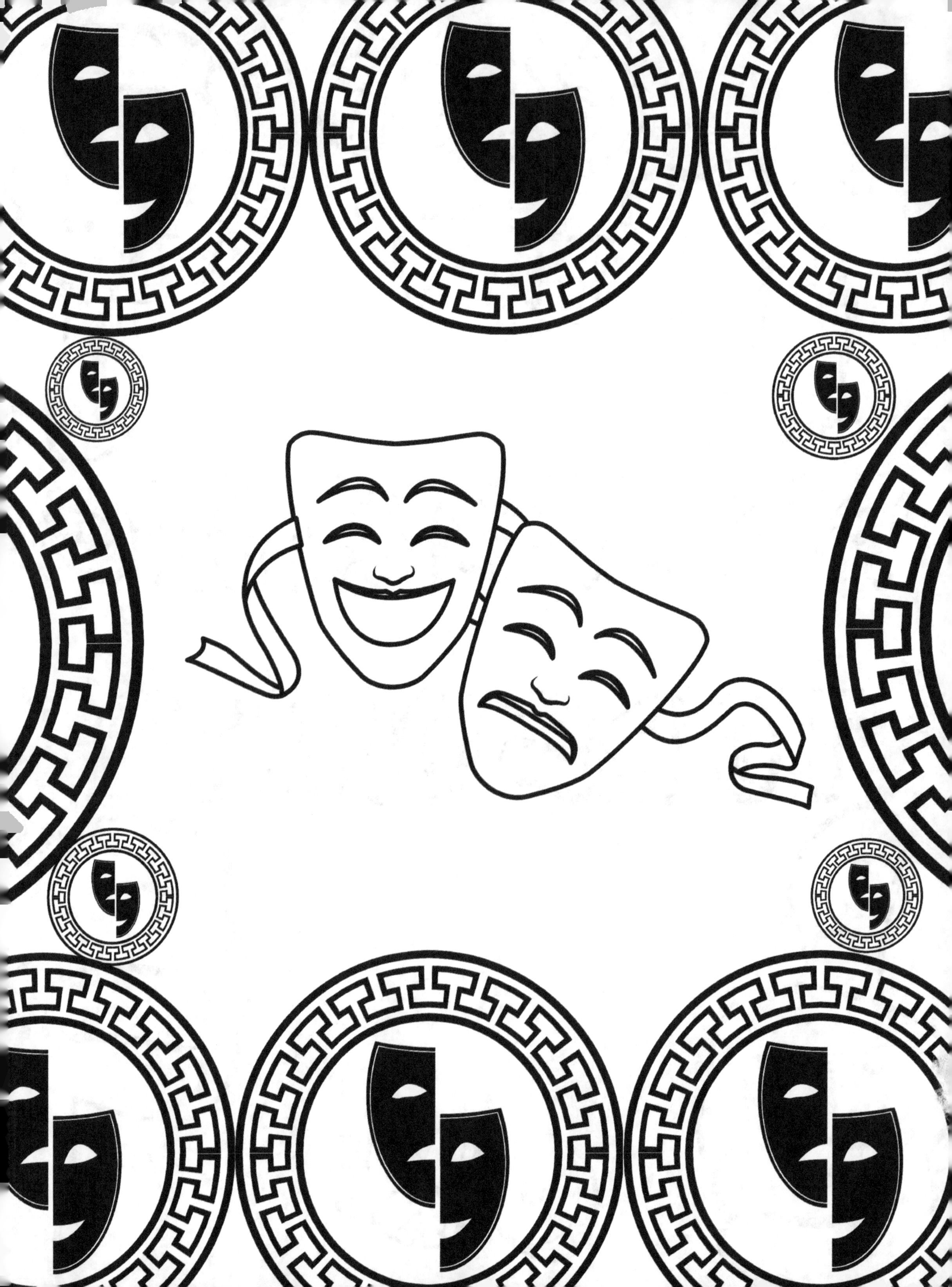

IN CASE NOBODY TOLD YOU,
IT IS OKAY TO NOT BE OKAY.
YOU DON'T GET A BEST ACTOR
AWARD FOR PRETENDING.

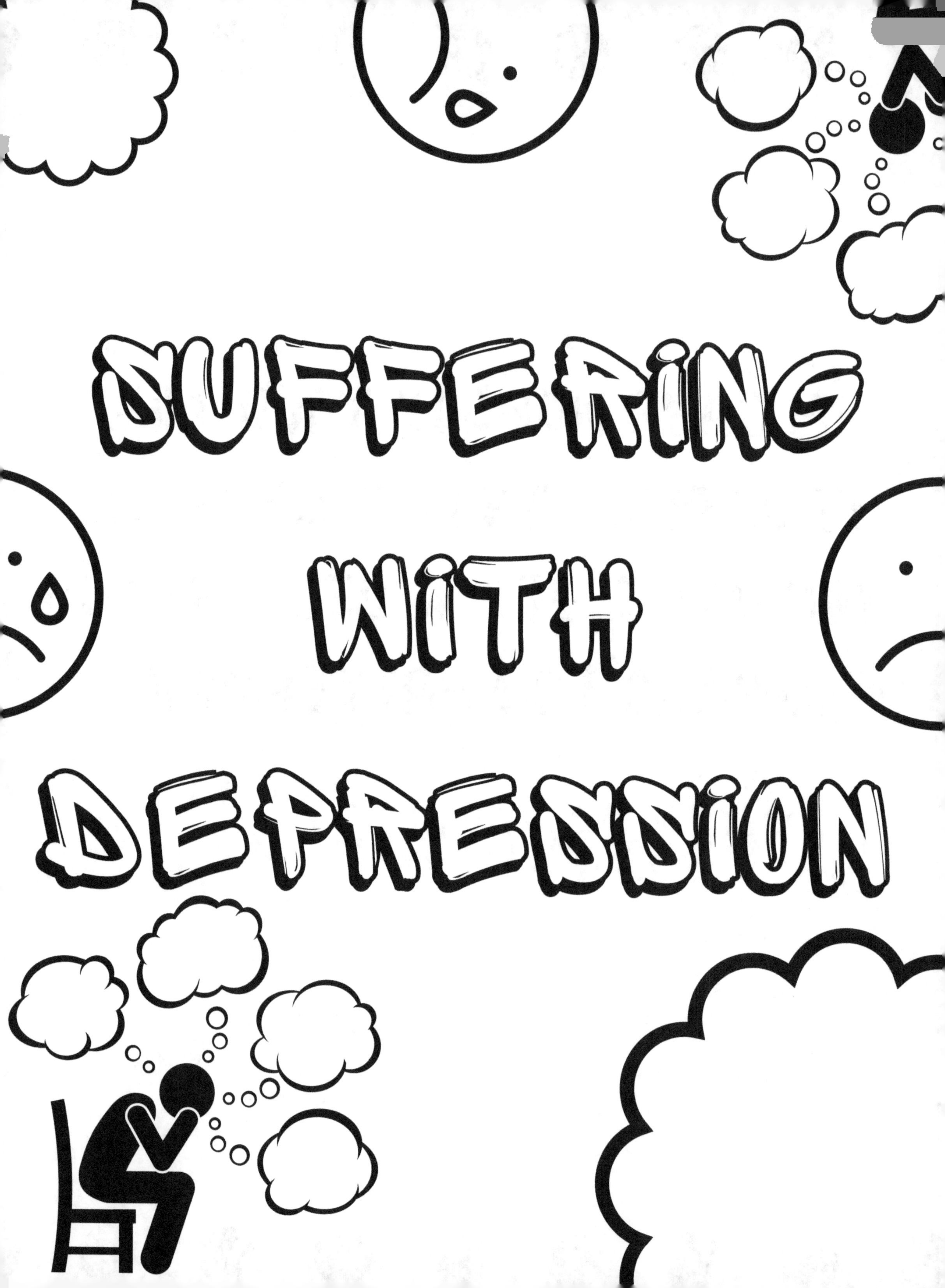
SUFFERING WITH DEPRESSION

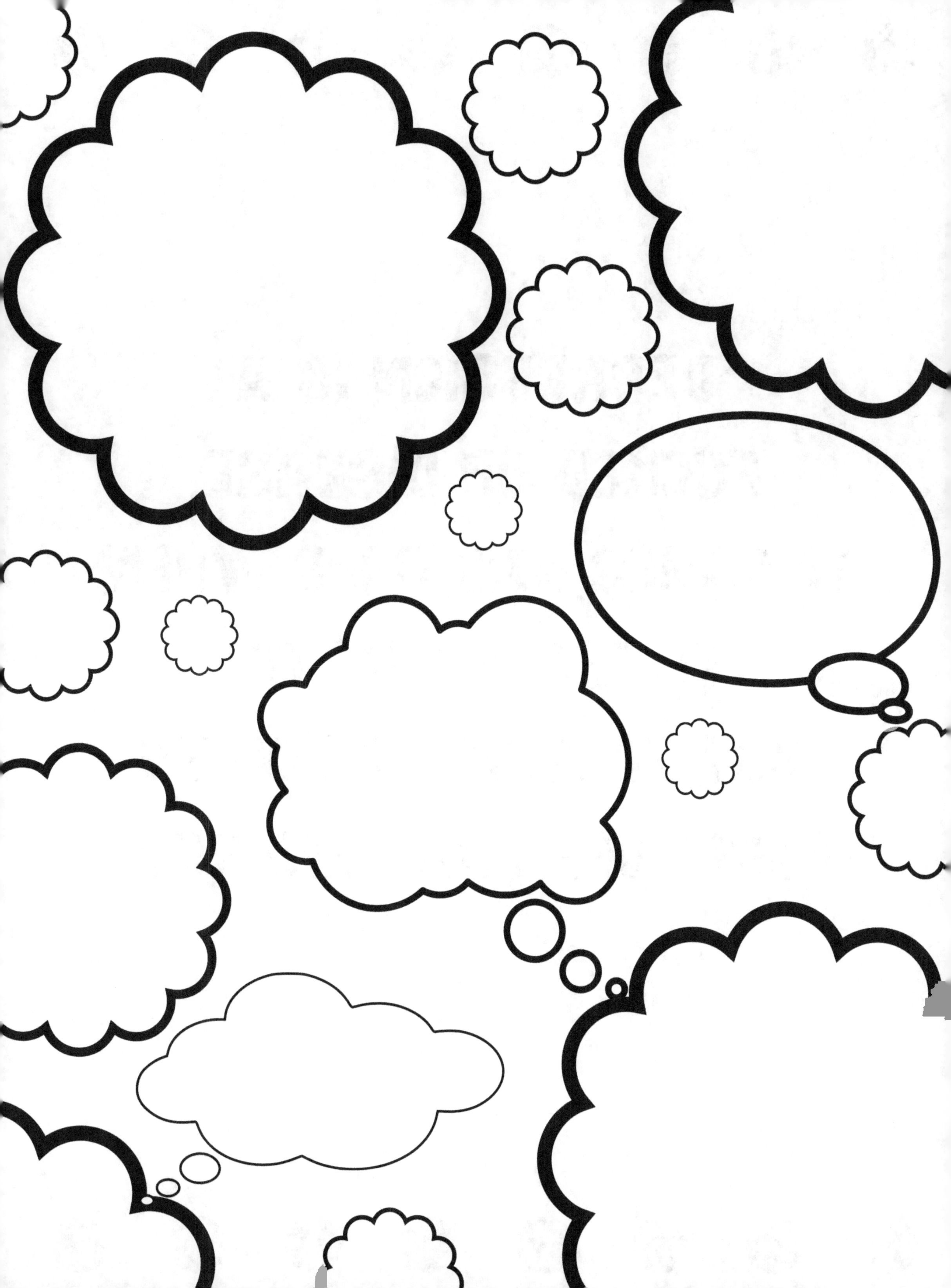

DEPRESSION IS A
FUCKED UP DISEASE.
IT COMES AND GOES WHEN
IT FEELS LIKE IT.
BUT IT IS UP TO YOU TO
FIGHT OFF THAT ENERGY.

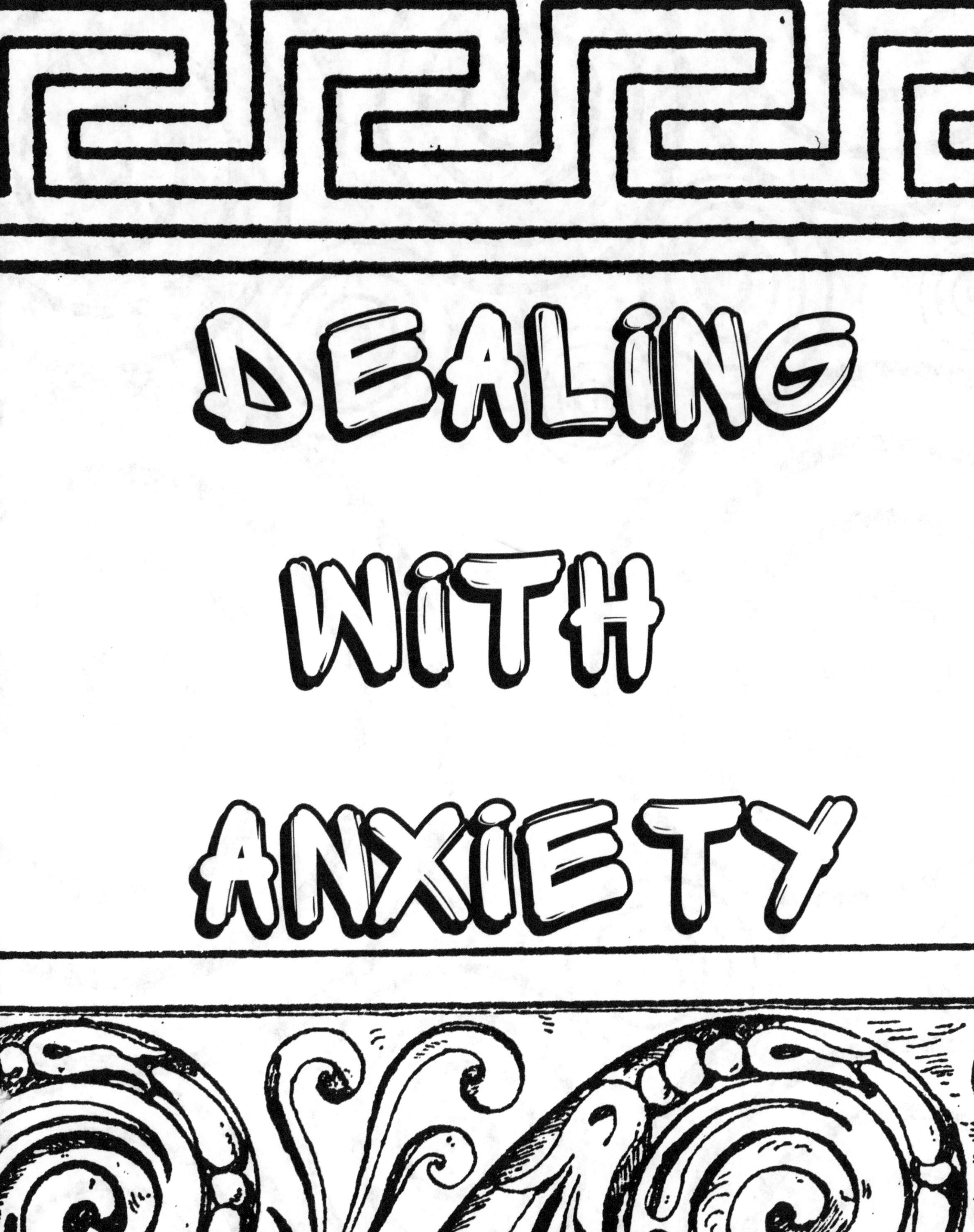

DEALING
WITH
ANXIETY

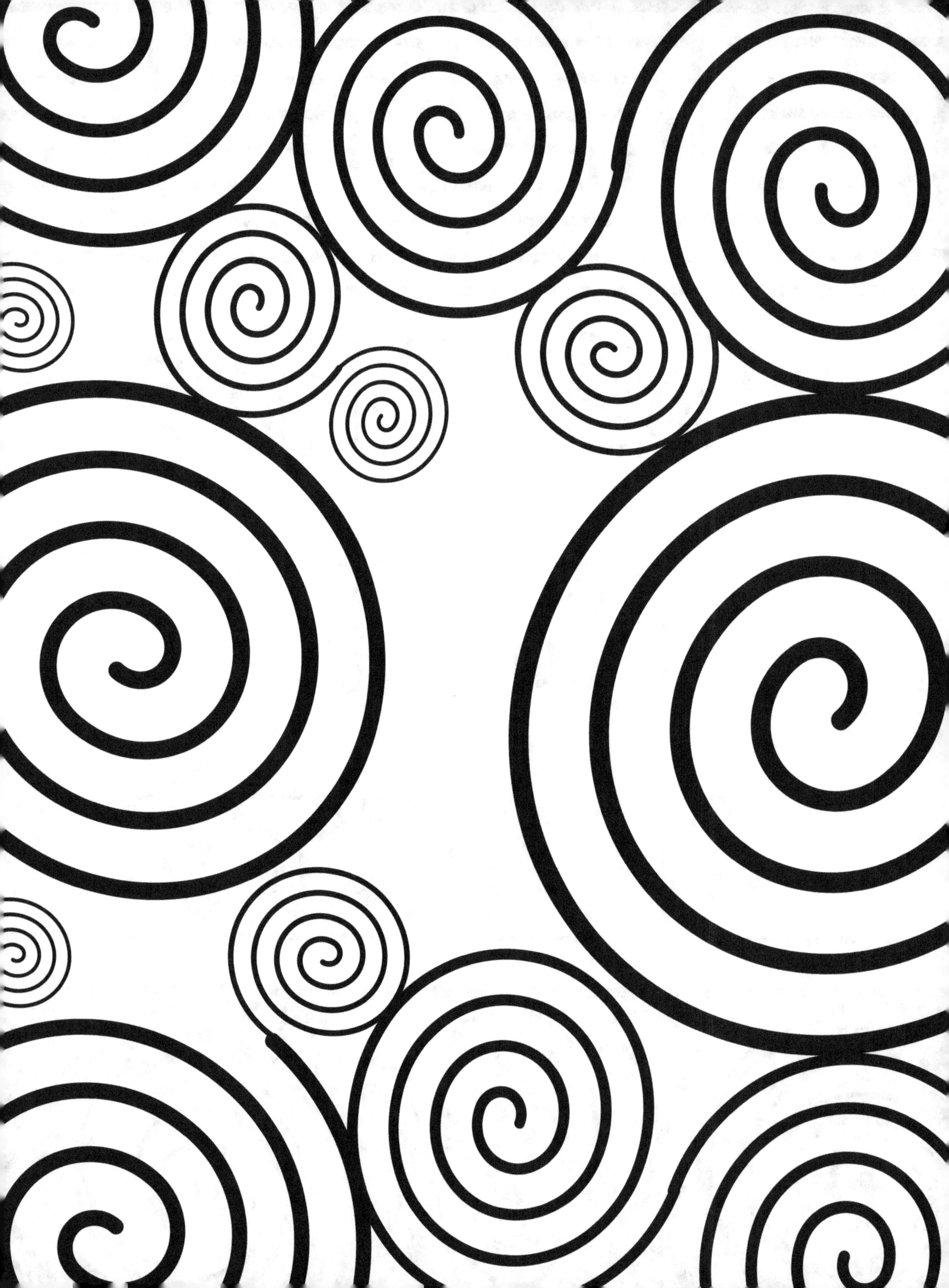

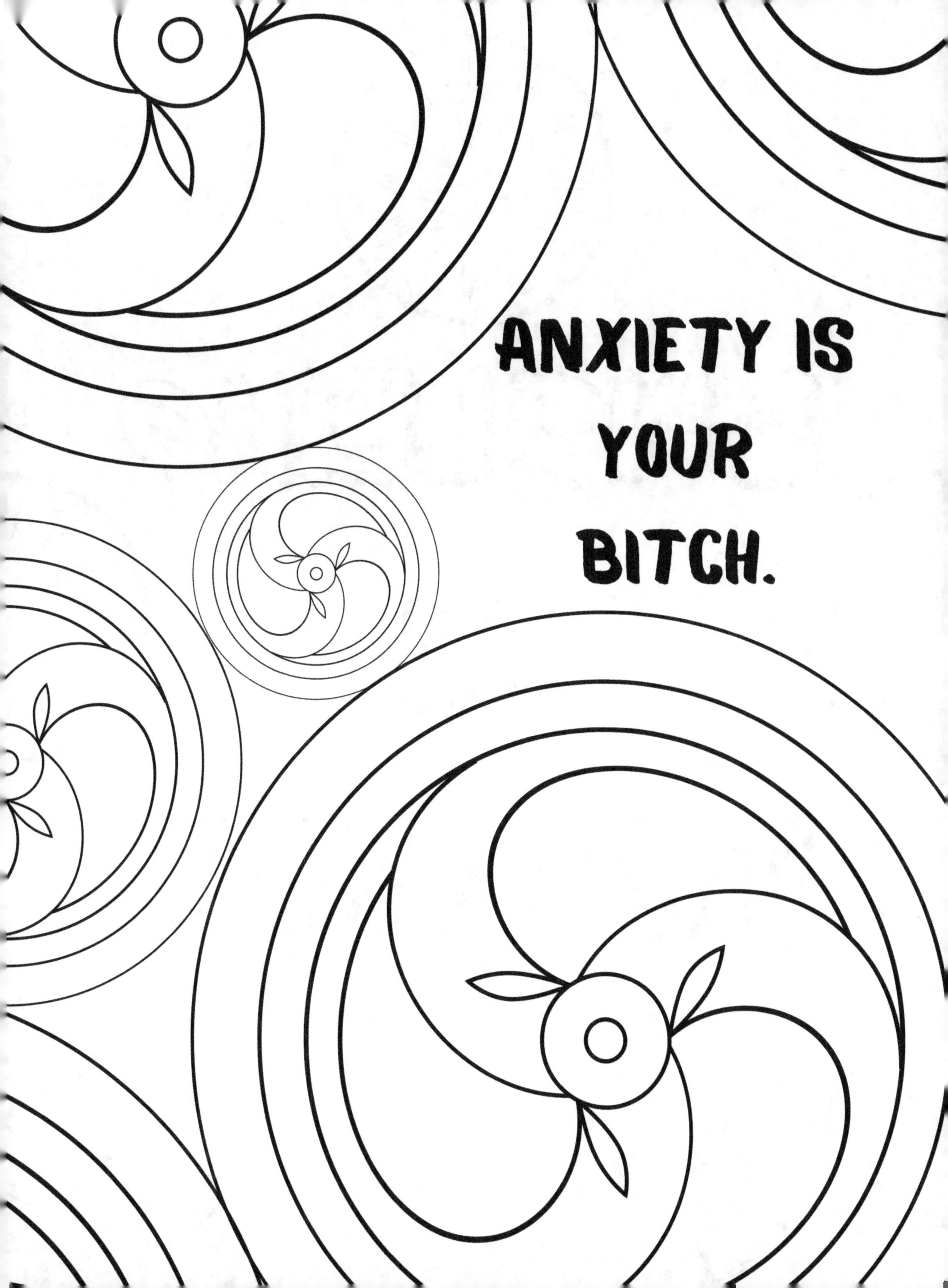

ANXIETY IS
YOUR
BITCH.

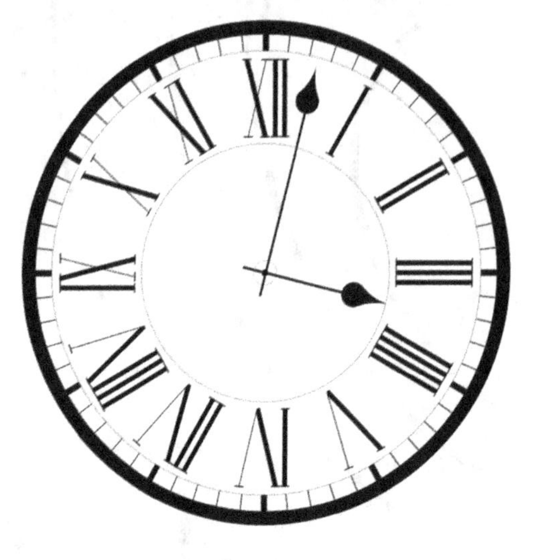

DWELLING

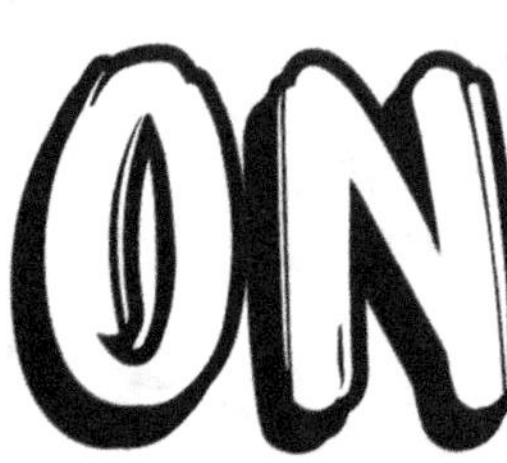

ON

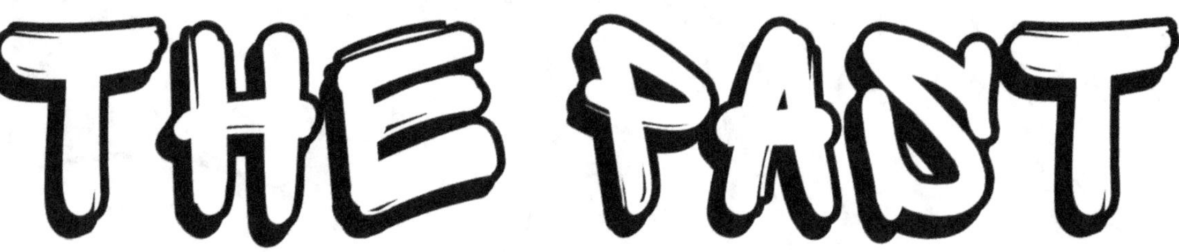

THE PAST

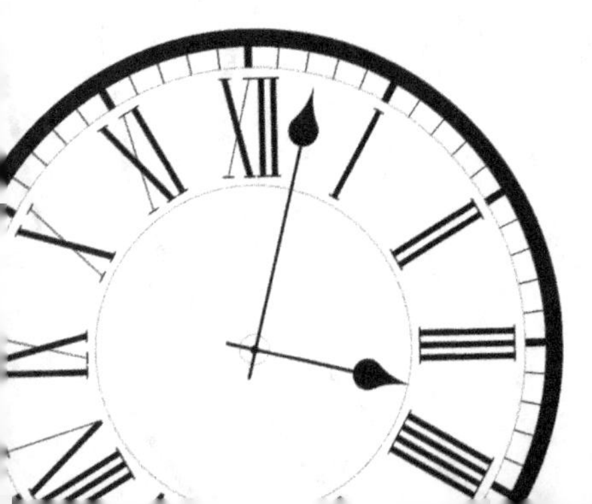

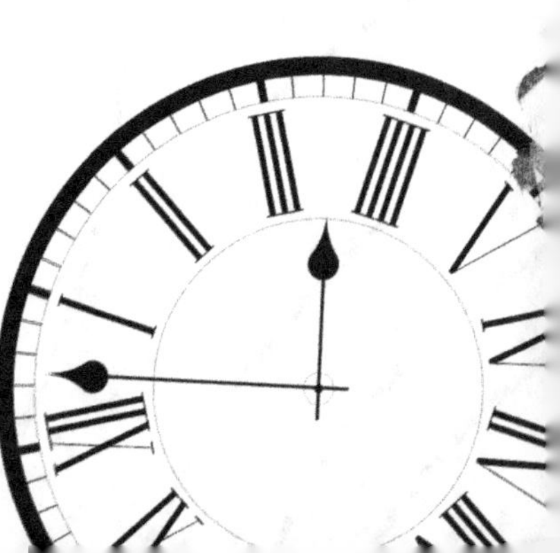

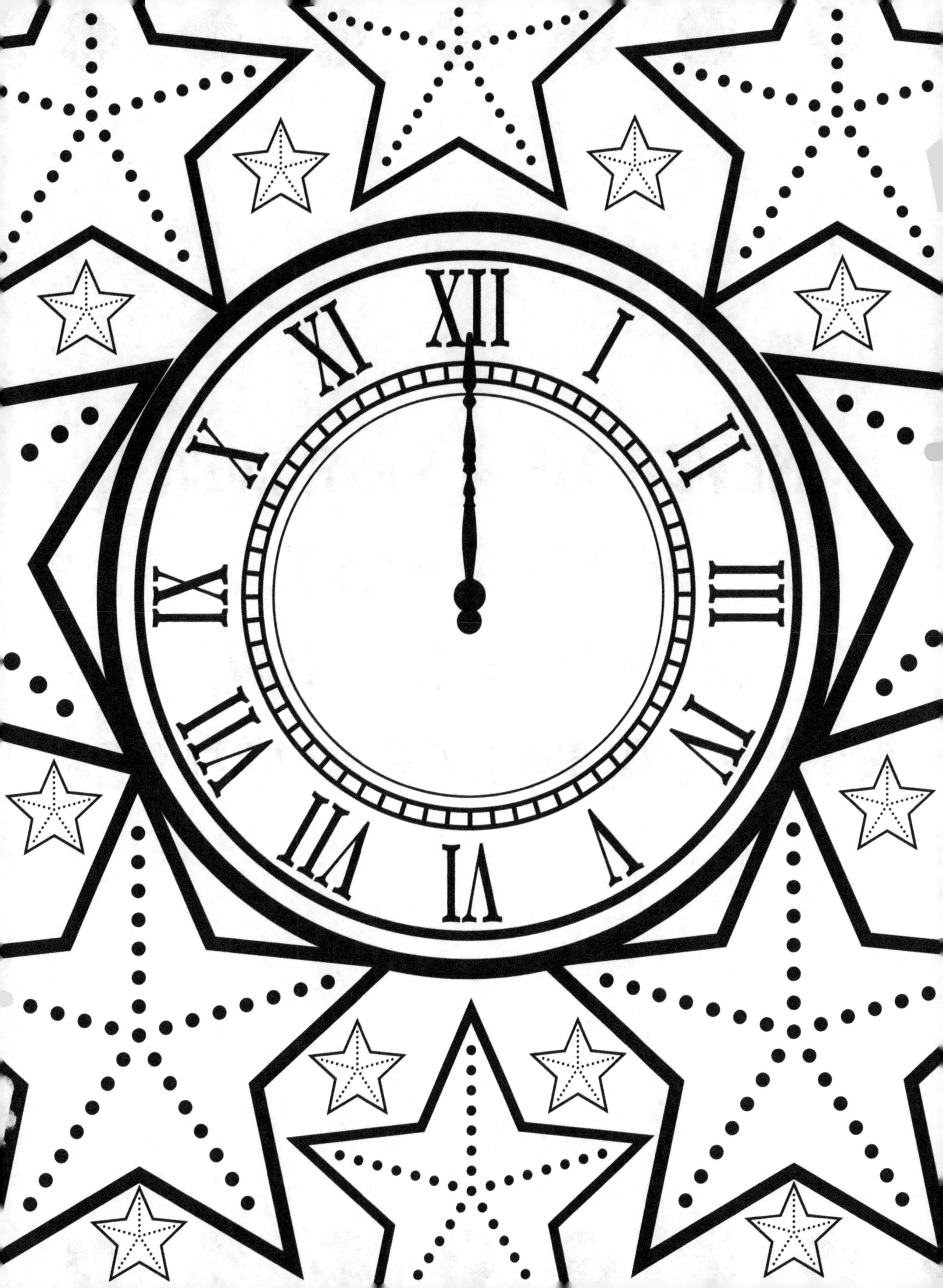

NEVER BE A PRISONER
OF YOUR PAST.
IT WAS A LESSON,
NOT A DAMN LIFE SENTENCE.

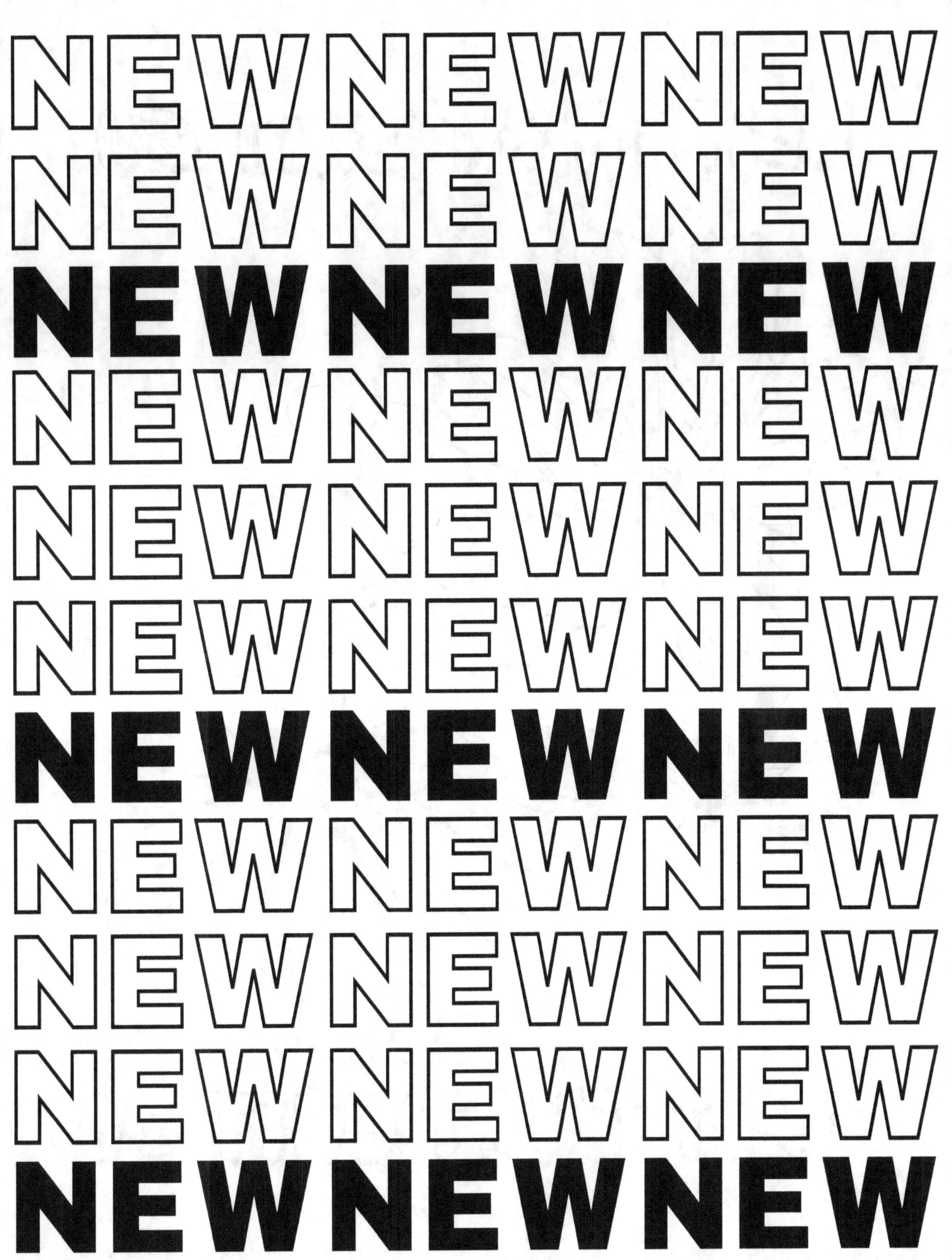

LET THAT SHIT GO

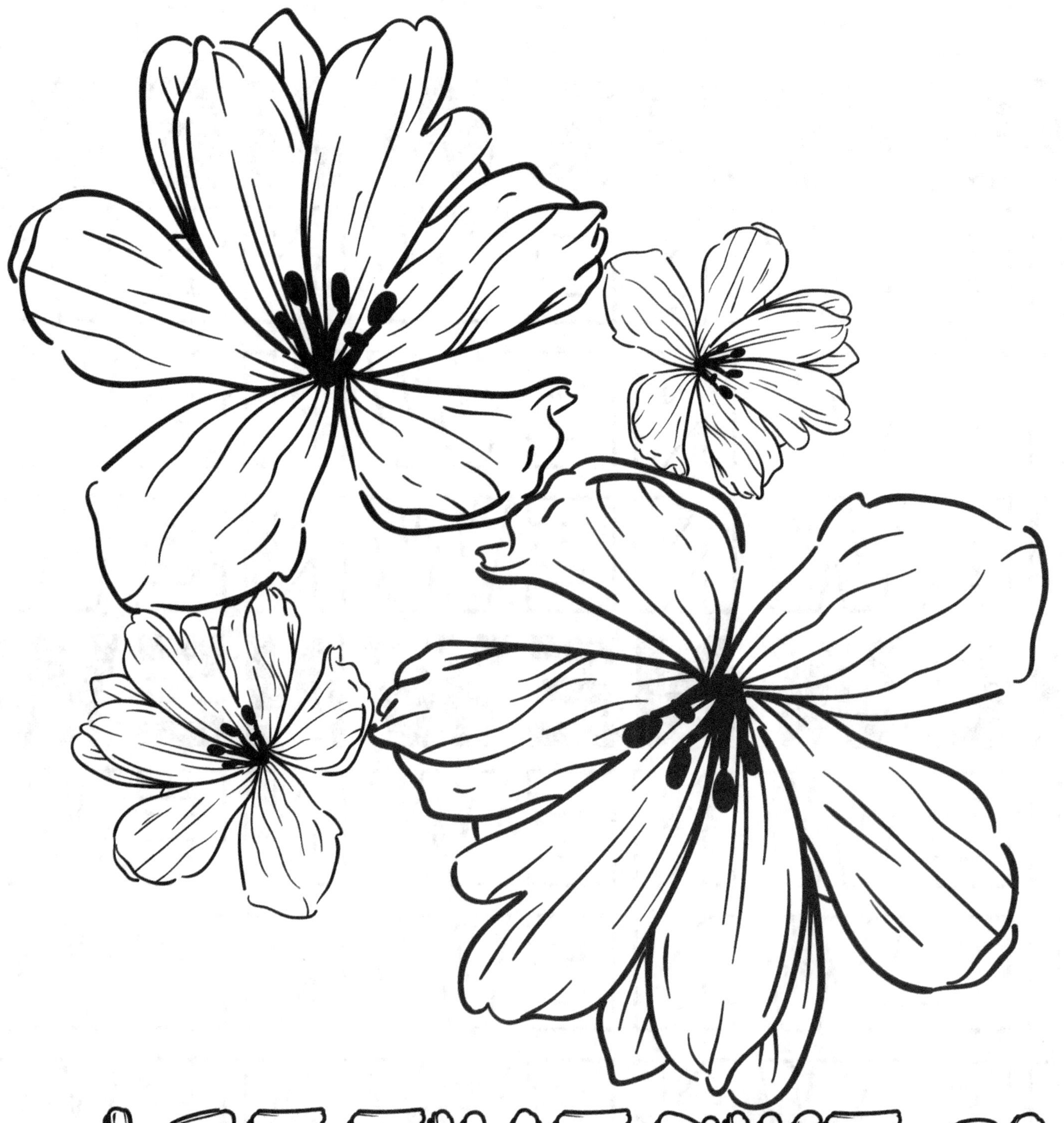

LET THAT SHIT GO

FUCK THAT EXTRA SHIT!
BE ALL ABOUT
POSITIVE MIND,
POSITIVE VIBES,
AND POSITIVE LIFE.

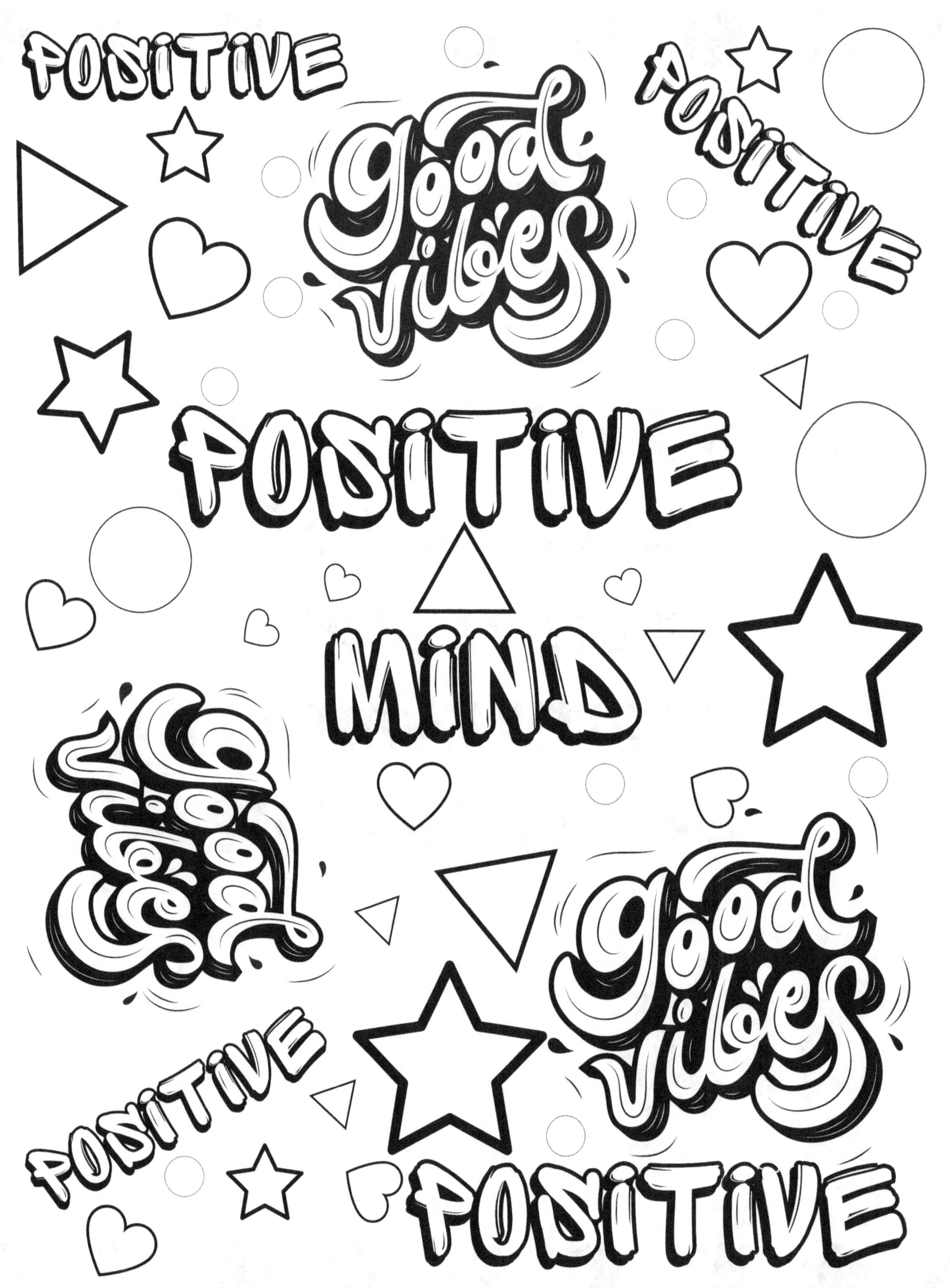

POSITIVE
good vibes
POSITIVE
POSITIVE
MIND
good vibes
POSITIVE
POSITIVE
POSITIVE

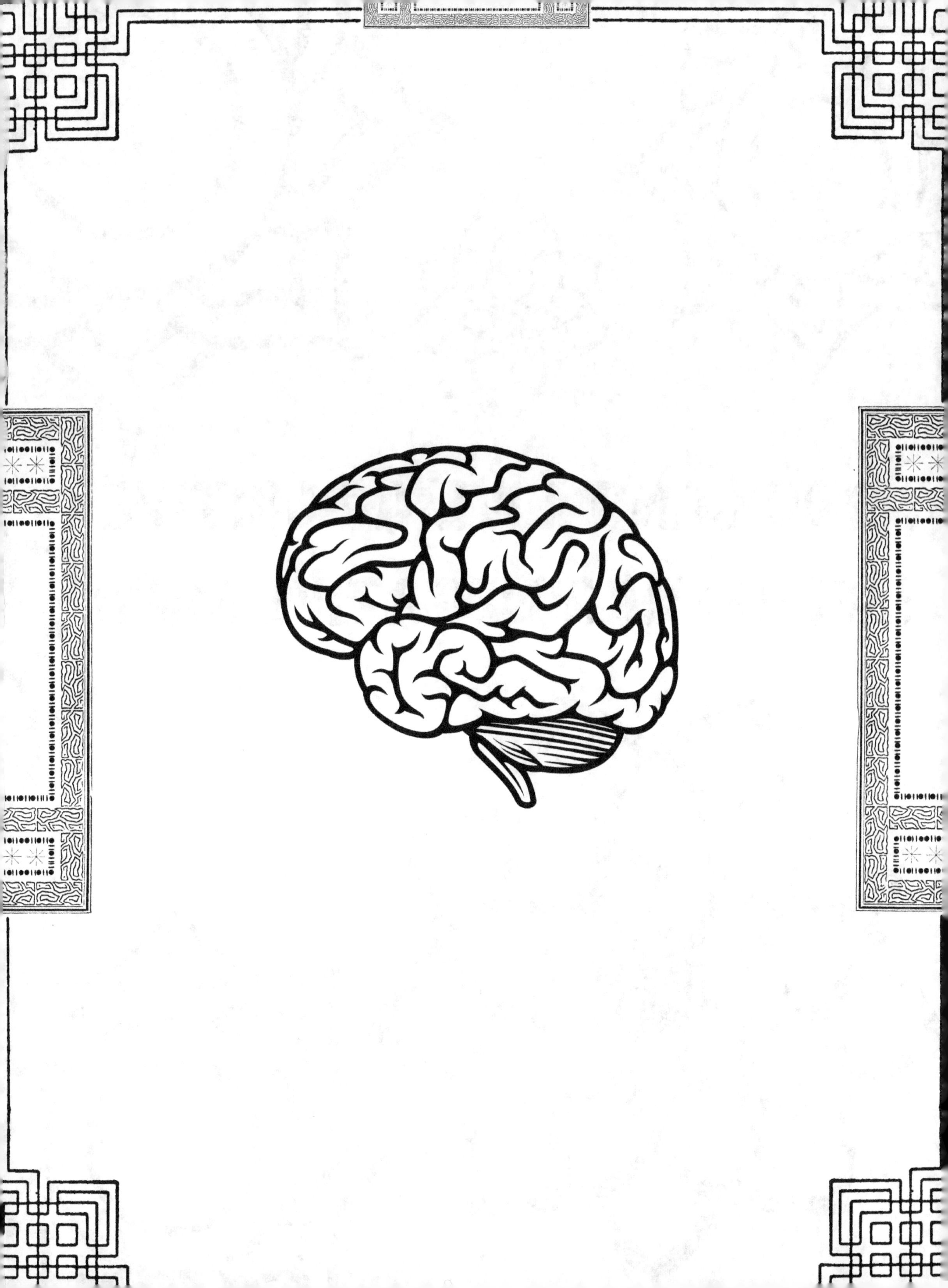

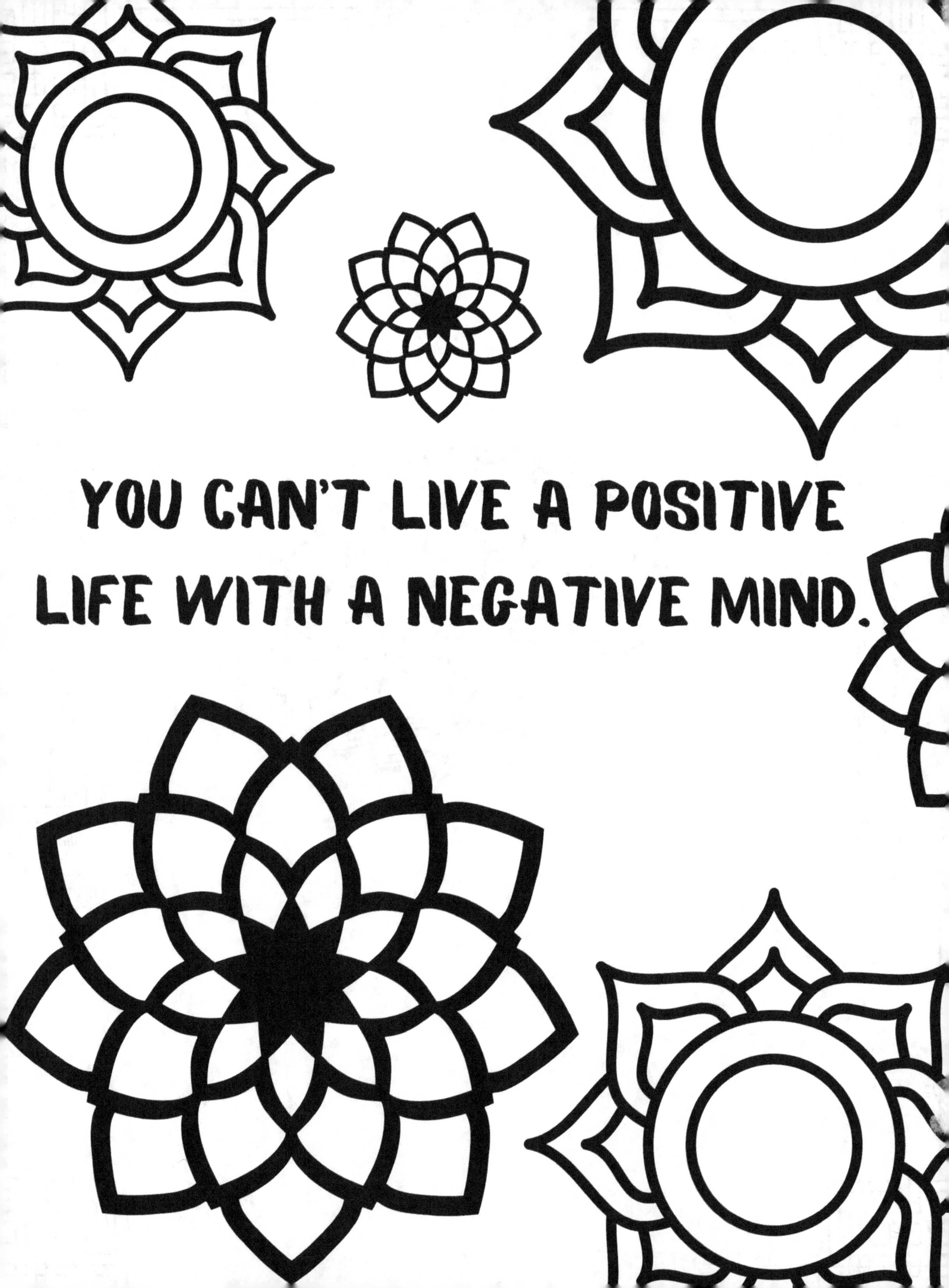

YOU CAN'T LIVE A POSITIVE
LIFE WITH A NEGATIVE MIND.

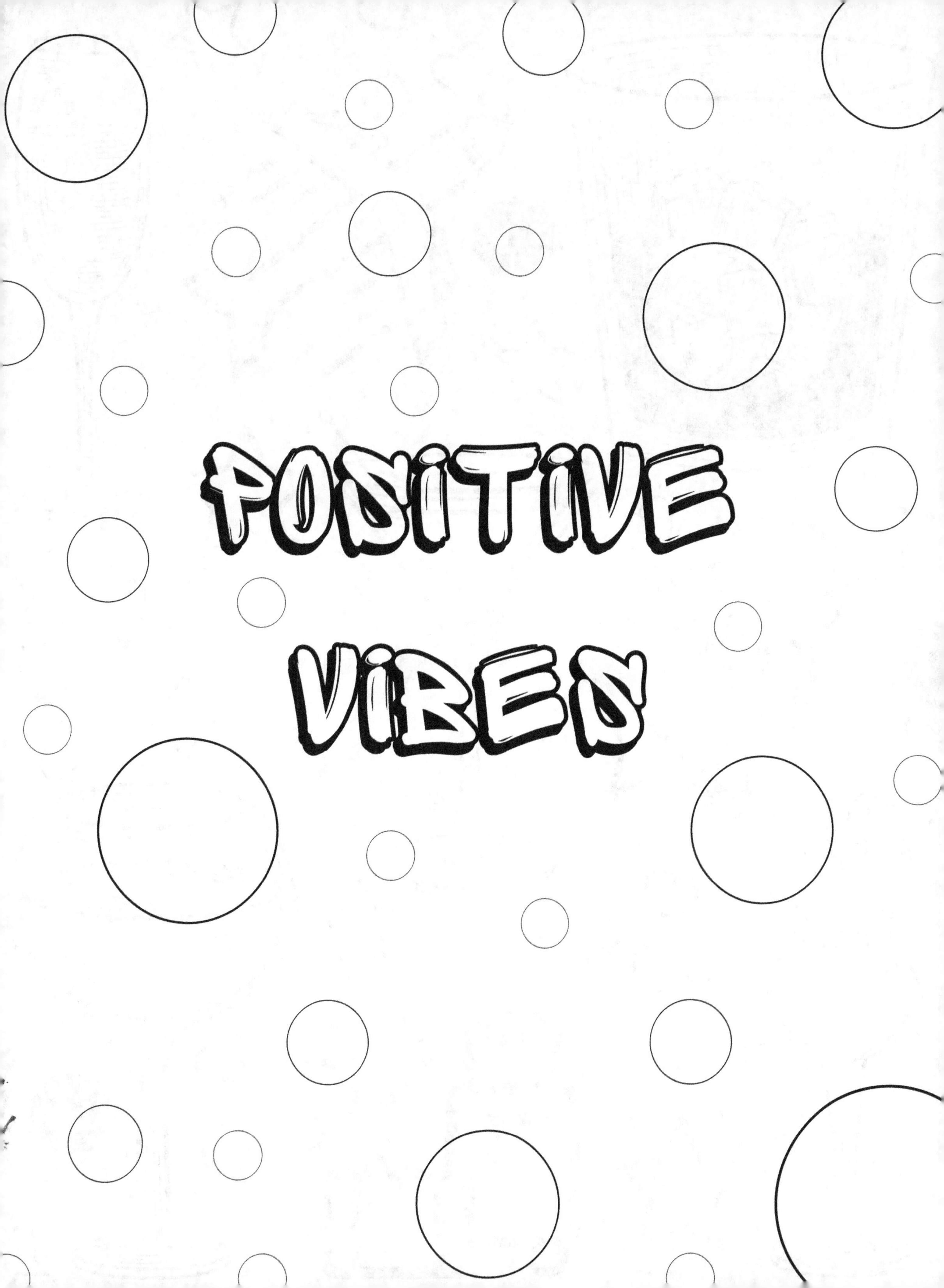

POSITIVE
VIBES

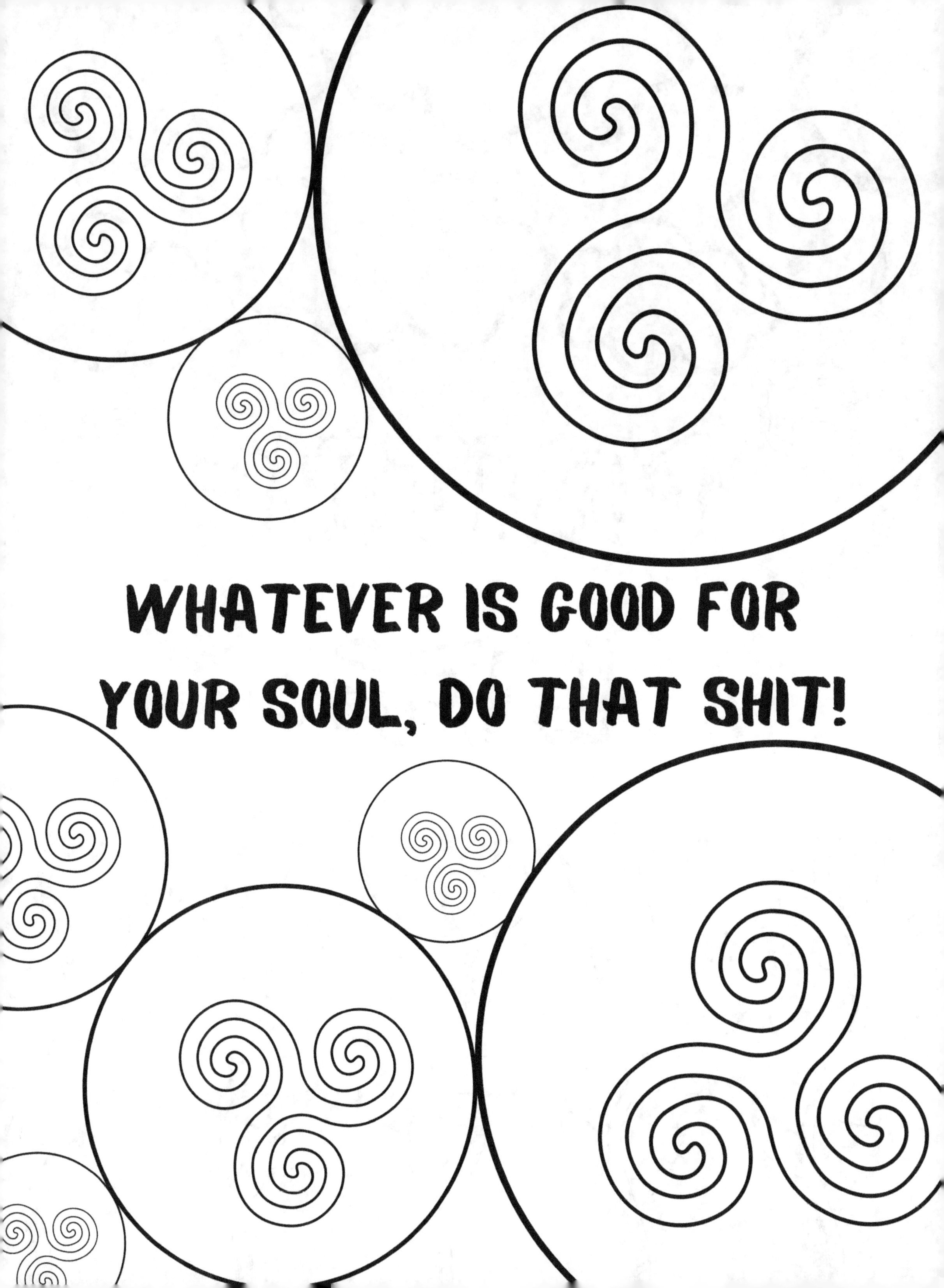

WHATEVER IS GOOD FOR
YOUR SOUL, DO THAT SHIT!

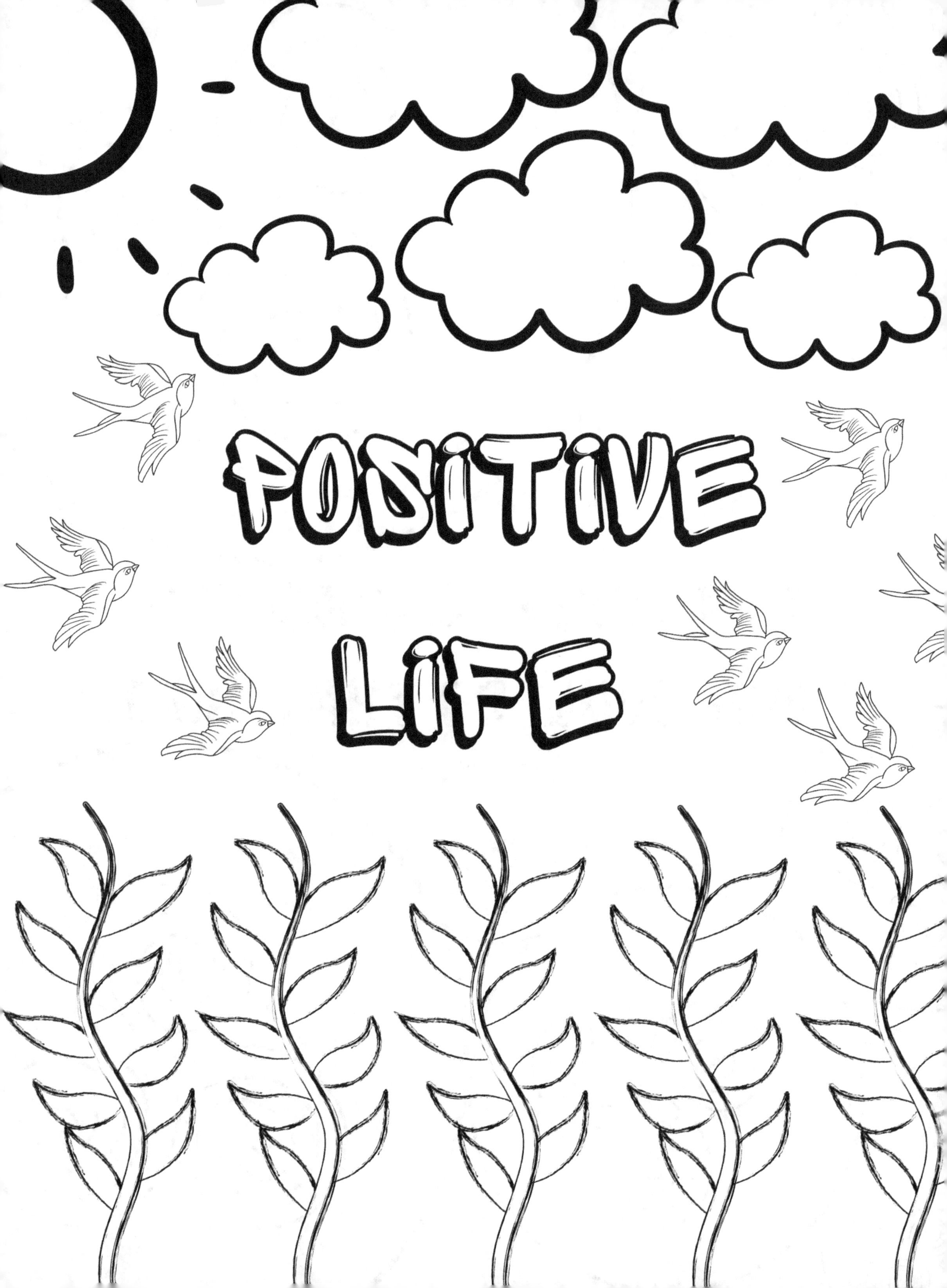

POSITIVE
LIFE

NO MORE JUST EXISTING.
IT IS TIME TO FUCKING LIVE.
AFTER ALL, YOU ARE THE
CEO OF YOUR LIFE.

RESOURCES

If you or someone you know is in a crisis, contact the Suicide Prevention Lifeline at 1-800-273-TALK (8255), or dial 911 in case of emergency.

If you or someone you know is experiencing a mental health or substance use problem, there are several resources available to assist. Check out some mental health resources below:

Substance Abuse and Mental Health Services Administration (SAMHSA)

U.S Department of Veterans Affairs (VA) — Mental Health

Anxiety and Depression Association of America (ADAA

National Alliance on Mental Illness (NAMI)

Depression and Bipolar Support Alliance

National Eating Disorders Association

American Psychiatry Association

National Institute on Aging

LGBT National Help Center

The Trevor Project

The Jed Foundation

Autism Speaks

www.ingramcontent.com/pod-product-compliance
Lightning Source LLC
Chambersburg PA
CBHW080524030726
47592CB00012B/3472